Heart and Soul

THE STORY OF FLORENCE NIGHTINGALE

Gena K. Gorrell

Tundra Books

Copyright © 2000 by Gena K. Gorrell
First Paperback Edition 2005

Published in Canada by Tundra Books,
481 University Avenue, Toronto, Ontario M5G 2E9

Published in the United States by Tundra Books of Northern New York,
P.O. Box 1030, Plattsburgh, New York 12901

Library of Congress Catalog Number: 00-131203

National Library of Canada Cataloguing in Publication

Gorrell, Gena K. (Gena Kinton), 1946-
    Heart and soul : the story of Florence Nightingale/Gena K. Gorrell.

Includes index.
ISBN 0-88776-494-0 (bound). – ISBN 0-88776-703-6 (pbk.)

I. Nightingale, Florence, 1820-1910 – Juvenile literature. 2. Nurses – England – Biography – Juvenile
literature. I. Title

RT37.N5G67 2000   j610.73'092   C00-930406-I

We acknowledge the financial support of the Government of Canada through the Book Publishing Industry
Development Program and that of the Government of Ontario through the Ontario Media Development
Corporation's Ontario Book Initiative. We further acknowledge the support of the Canada Council for the
Arts and the Ontario Arts Council for our publishing program.

Design by Ingrid Paulson

Printed and bound in Canada

1 2 3 4 5 6   10 09 08 07 06 05

Heart and Soul

CONTENTS

For map, see pages 58–59

INTRODUCTION

N THE TWENTY-FIRST CENTURY, MOST OF US LIVING IN developed countries take good health for granted. We assume that, if we get sick or injured, we'll go to a clinic or hospital and the doctors and nurses will cure us, or at least make us feel better. We expect to live into old age. When someone dies young, we see it as a shocking tragedy.

We are very, ~~very lucky~~

Just a few generations ago – in my great-grandparents' lifetime – illness and premature death were an inescapable part of family life. Many women died in childbirth, and commonly girls and boys did not live beyond childhood. Tides of contagious diseases – typhus, tuberculosis, smallpox, cholera, influenza – swept through the population, killing tens of thousands. Two or three members of a family might die in the space of a week. But it didn't take an epidemic to kill people; even a small cut or scratch could lead to a fatal infection.

Why was life so perilous? Very little was known about health, and even less about medicine. Physicians and surgeons were trained in a hodgepodge of traditional "cures" based on superstitions and ancient theories, but often they had no understanding of the problems they were trying to treat. People didn't know where infections came from, or how to stop them from spreading, and there were no antibiotics to cure them.

If you were sick in those days, you stayed at home, and the women in your family did their best to keep you clean and warm. They fixed you special meals of nourishing, easily digestible food. They applied hot or cold compresses (cloths) to whatever part of you ached. They sat with you, comforted you, read to you, and prayed for your recovery.

Hospitals existed, but they weren't for curing people. You went to hospital if you had nowhere else to go, and no one to care for you. Some hospitals were run by churches, and their patients were cared for by nuns. Others depended on medical students, and on so-called nurses who had no medical training. Some hospitals were well run and fairly comfortable, and others were horrible. Either way, though, the result was usually the same. If you went into a hospital, you probably wouldn't come out alive.

In less than two hundred years, hospitals and health care and the entire medical profession have changed beyond recognition. A great many people brought about the changes, but a few of them stand out as pioneers whose vision and inspiration saved countless lives, and brought us benefits beyond measure.

This is the story of one of them.

A Word of Explanation

The nations and boundaries of Europe changed repeatedly during the eighteenth and nineteenth centuries. For simplicity's sake, I have generally referred to countries by the names now applied to the regions – Germany, Italy, and so on.

A BIRTH IN FIRENZE

Let children that would fear the Lord
Hear what their teachers say:
With reverence hear their parent's word,
And with delight obey.

Have you not heard what dreadful plagues
Are threaten'd by the Lord,
To him that breaks his father's laws,
Or mocks his mother's word?

What heavy guilt upon him lies!
How cursed is his name!
The ravens shall pick out his eyes,
And eagles eat the same.
    – Divine and Moral Songs for Children, circa 1715

N MAY 12, IN THE YEAR 1820, A BABY GIRL WAS BORN IN THE Italian city of Firenze. Her parents were not Italian; they were a young English couple, William and Fanny Nightingale. The pair already had a one-year-old daughter, born in the Italian city of

Naples and called Parthenope (Par-THEN-oh-pee, from the Greek for "maidenly" or "pure"), after an ancient Greek colony at that site. The Nightingales decided that their new baby should have an equally unusual name. She too would be called after her birthplace.

In English, Firenze is called Florence.

William Nightingale was twenty-five years old when Florence was born. He was a tall, thin young man, intelligent, thoughtful, and bookish. He was the son of a successful banker, and he could have achieved a great deal himself. But the young man was indolent by nature and, since he had inherited a fortune from an uncle, he had no need to apply his talents. His marriage to Fanny Smith, a lively, strong-willed woman six years his senior, only increased his laziness.

Fanny came from a family known for its wealth and good deeds. Her grandfather Samuel Smith had made a lot of money in the grocery business, and he was a strong supporter of good causes. As a Member of Parliament, her father, William Smith, had fought against slavery and the oppression of the poor. Like her relatives, Fanny was energetic and opinionated. One of ten children, she had grown up in a whirl of picnics and parties, dances, and amateur theatricals; she loved comfort and good company.

The couple had set out on their tour of Europe two years earlier, just after their wedding. Napoleon and his armies had finally been defeated in 1815, after more than twenty years of European war, and Britain's rich families were flocking back to the Continent. They traveled in horse-drawn coaches, accompanied by valets, grooms, uniformed footmen, cooks, maids, and nannies, and cartloads of baggage. They stayed in luxury hotels or rented spacious villas; they toured museums, palaces, and cathedrals; they nibbled at elegant luncheons and ate their way through ten-course dinners. They exhausted themselves sightseeing, shopping, and dancing at gala balls, and restored themselves in the natural hot springs of spas or at fashionable seaside resorts.

In 1821, when Florence was one year old, her parents decided to go back to

Fanny Nightingale was a clever, beautiful woman, and a wonderful hostess. But she did not share the humanitarian zeal of her father and grandfather; she loved fun and fashion. She herself said, "We Smiths never thought of anything all day long but our own ease and pleasure."

England. William would happily have stayed in Italy, reading and visiting and doing nothing in particular, but Fanny was ambitious. She wanted to live in a fine home, entertain important people, and be a grand lady. William's inheritance included some land, with a lead mine and smelter, in the county of Derbyshire. (Lead was smelted, or melted and purified, and used to make such products as ammunition, plumbing pipes, and pewter dishes.) He designed a handsome new house for his family – a mansion with fifteen bedrooms, and a beautiful garden of stone terraces, and a wonderful view of a river – and they named it Lea Hurst. (A lea is a meadow, and a hurst is a low hill.) There they settled down to raise their two daughters, in the heart of England.

Lea Hurst, where Florence lived as a small child. Although the Nightingales soon moved to a larger house, they kept Lea Hurst as a summer retreat. Surrounded by hills, moors, and pretty little villages, it remained Florence's favorite home.

It was a time of great changes. Just a few months before Florence was born, King George III had died, after sixty years on the throne. When he was crowned, back in 1760, Great Britain had been a mostly agricultural society. Wealthy landowners controlled vast areas of forest and farmland. Some of these owners were nobility – dukes and duchesses, lords and ladies – and others were "landed gentry," families who might not have titles but who could trace their ancestors and estates back for centuries.

The landowners rented out some of their land to tenant farmers, and employed servants, laborers, and craftsmen to do the work on the rest of their property: tending livestock, growing crops, constructing buildings, making clothes and tools, cooking and housekeeping. Many of the items used on the estate were produced there. Travel, by horseback, cart, or carriage, was slow and uncomfortable, and it was not uncommon for laborers to live out their lives without ever leaving the neighborhood where they'd been born. Both the mansion and the worker's cottage were heated (barely) by fires of wood or coal, and lit (feebly) by oil lamps or candles. Almost all work was done by hand, as it had been for hundreds of years.

Around the mid-1700s, all this began to change. A host of new inventions and technologies overturned Britain's traditional farming life, in an upheaval that we call the Industrial Revolution.

Inventors worked out how to use the steam from boiling water to drive machinery. The new steam engines made coal mining much more efficient, so more coal was available to boil more water in more steam engines. Steam engines and other new machines soon replaced much of the manual labor on country estates. Jobs that had been done by hand – like combing and dyeing wool, spinning cotton into thread, or weaving thread into cloth or stockings – could now be done mechanically. In 1850 the commercial sewing machine was invented, to churn out fine stitching far faster than any poor seamstress working by candlelight.

As workers moved from the fields and open air into dark, crowded factories, industrial towns grew into cities, and cities sprawled into slums. Between 1800 and 1880, the population of London grew from one million to more than four million, as workers crammed their families into filthy, squalid tenement buildings. Meanwhile, the people who owned the factories were making fortunes, as Britain's wealth came more and more from its industry.

There was no shortage of raw material for the factories. Although some of the North American colonies broke away from Britain during George III's reign, to form the United States of America, Britain still owned territories

In 1821 these mail coaches carried passengers for a fare, as buses do today. While some people were crammed inside the coach, others paid less and perched outside. Bad weather was only one of the risks; passengers were often injured as a result of "overturns, violent driving, horses proceeding without drivers, drunken coachmen, overloading, breaking down, and racing."

around the world. Where the British didn't hold political power, they often had profitable trading arrangements instead. British ships brought wool from Australia and New Zealand; cotton, spices, and dyes from India; furs and whale products from Canada; cotton and sugar from the Caribbean; gold,

The Industrial Revolution increased Britain's wealth and power, but it forced many workers – including young children – to trade their outdoor farming life for long, boring days in gloomy, often dangerous factories. While steam locomotives thundered through once-peaceful valleys, graceful towns were defaced by blocks of factories, and industrial pollution fouled the rivers, fields, and skies. In an 1854 novel, Charles Dickens described such a scene: "It was a town of machinery and tall chimneys, out of which interminable serpents of smoke trailed themselves for ever and ever, and never got uncoiled. It had a black canal in it, and a river that ran purple with ill-smelling dye, and vast piles of buildings full of windows where there was a rattling and a trembling all day long. . . ."

diamonds, and mahogany from Africa; rubber from South America; silks and spices from the Far East. As these precious cargoes arrived on Britain's doorstep, many were turned into luxury goods to be sold at home or around the world.

❧

The new technology soon spread beyond the workplace. Gas lighting was first installed in factories, but by 1815 there were twenty-six miles (42 km) of pipes carrying gas to light up London's streetlamps, public buildings, and even some wealthy homes. Steam locomotives were invented to move coal around the mines, but by 1825 they were starting to pull passenger trains, taking people farther in an hour or two than a horse could take them in a day. Steam technology and other new processes led to higher-quality iron, which meant better tools, machines, bridges, and boats.

In 1820 an iron steamship crossed the English Channel to France, and by 1838 steamships were crossing the Atlantic three times as fast as a sailing-ship could. By 1845 an underwater telegraph cable transmitted Morse code messages between England and France, and twenty years later a similar cable reached all the way to America. These developments brought countries closer together, making foreign trade and travel faster and cheaper. People's lives and attitudes were being drastically altered, and the old rules of society were being upset.

❧

One great distinction between the upper and lower classes had been the fact that ladies and gentlemen *did not work*. There were exceptions – a gentleman could hold a post (preferably a high one) in the church or army or government, and a lady could volunteer her services to a worthy cause. But if you had a regular job – such as making things or selling things – you didn't belong to "society."

Society families enjoy Regent's Park in the 1820s. In this fashionable part of London, even the small children are elaborately dressed. The soldier toward the right is a reminder that Britain had recently been at war with France and the United States.

With the world changing, though, ordinary people – people whose parents and grandparents had been workers – were making fortunes out of their businesses. They were buying great houses, and going to theaters and balls, and traveling first-class, and bringing up their children to be ladies and gentlemen. At first these "new rich" were snubbed as *parvenus* (French for "just got here"). As they became richer and more powerful, they were gradually accepted into society. But their status was insecure. If they did the wrong things, or even knew the wrong people, they could be cold-shouldered out of the fashionable world.

The Nightingales were part of this new gentry. They were wealthy and cultured, they were connected to important people, they were too influential to be ignored. But they were still "new money." If they wanted to move in the "best circles," they must have no more jobs, no more careers. To be part of society, they must live by society's rules.

They could hardly imagine that little Florence was going to make up rules of her own.

CHAPTER TWO

FLO AND PARTHE

Q. What ought a well-educated girl to have learnt at 15?

A. She ought to read freely in prose or verse; to write grammatically; to be very expert in arithmetic; to know French and Italian; to be familiar with geography, history, and biography; to be mistress of approved and desirable accomplishments; and, above all, to be ready at all kinds of needlework.
– The Mother's Question Book, circa 1850

ANNY NIGHTINGALE SOON DECIDED THAT LEA HURST, with its fifteen bedrooms, was too small, cold, and remote to be the family's only house. By the time Florence was five years old, the family had bought a handsome manor called Embley Park, near Portsmouth and the south coast. Lea Hurst, with its cool breezes and fine view, became their summer home.

Embley was nearer to the excitement of London. It was also conveniently close to two of Fanny's sisters, so young Flo and Parthe could share visits and parties with two sets of cousins: the very wealthy Nicholsons and the well-connected Bonham Carters. Other cousins came to stay at Embley, and the two girls grew up in a flurry of guests, games, pets, excursions, and other amusements.

At Embley Park, the Nightingales' imposing new home, the family enjoyed a luxurious life. The estate covered more than four thousand acres (1600 ha) of fields and forests.

There was also plenty of schoolwork. William Nightingale might lack initiative for himself, but he insisted that his daughters be exceptionally well educated. At first Flo and Parthe had governesses, but when Florence was twelve her father took over most of their education. He patiently tutored them in classical Latin and Greek, and in French, Italian, and German. They read great books in the original languages. He also had them study history, philosophy, ethics, composition, mathematics, and the Bible.

Parthe was often jealous of her domineering little sister, who was better at schoolwork, prettier and wittier, and clearly their father's favorite. But if William had special feelings for his clever younger daughter, Fanny preferred her older child. In her view, studying wasn't all that important. After all, girls didn't grow up to have careers; they got married and had babies and ran households. A properly brought-up girl had to be reasonably well educated so she could make a good impression in society. She needed to be clever and amusing so she would be popular. But beyond that, how much book learning did she need?

Parthe was more Fanny's idea of a normal daughter. She was sociable rather than scholarly. She liked talking and visiting, and planning wonderful parties, and helping her mother with needlework, flower-arranging, letter-writing, and the many other tasks of a country lady.

"All young ladies accomplished! My dear Charles, what do you mean?"

"Yes, all of them, I think. They all paint tables, cover skreens and net purses. I scarcely know any one who cannot do all this, and I am sure I never heard a young lady spoken of for the first time, without being informed that she was very accomplished."

In her 1815 novel *Pride and Prejudice*, Jane Austen mocks the education of most fashionable young women of her day. Girls learned show-off skills to impress suitors, and memorized lists of facts they were hardly likely to need – such as "all the Metals, Semi-Metals, Planets, and distinguished philosophers." They practiced singing, dancing, and playing an instrument. They sketched portraits and painted landscapes. They spent hours on needlework, plain and fancy. But they were seldom asked to stretch their minds with new or difficult ideas, let alone venture into original thought.

Florence (seated) and Parthenope, when Florence was sixteen. She was slim and graceful, with a fine complexion and glossy reddish hair, but she was certainly not the placid china doll suggested by this painting.

But Flo! She was often a stubborn, brooding, unhappy child. Worse yet, sometimes she hardly seemed to be in the same world. She was a dreamer, always drifting off into fantasies. As a young child, Florence later wrote, she was sure she was different from other people. She felt guilty about being different, and she was terrified that people would find out, and see her as a monster. As she grew up, she became more and more of a misfit, ducking the social life around her, dreaming of doing heroic deeds. She was frustrated by the narrowness of her world, and bored by the shallow chitchat and gossip of family visits.

One relative she did care for was Mai Smith. Mai was her aunt twice over: she was William's younger sister, and she had married Fanny's brother Sam. When Flo was eleven, Mai gave birth to a son, Shore Smith, and Florence adored him too – "my boy Shore," she called him. She would always be fond of babies.

As she grew into her teenage years, Florence enjoyed her schoolwork, and had a close and affectionate relationship with her father. They were both lonely by nature – studious and serious-minded, given to reading and deep reflection. They could be moody and particular, even nit-picking. Neither one of them was comfortable in the nonstop social whirl that Fanny created at Embley Park.

With her intelligence, good looks, and fashionable family, Florence would be courted by any number of eligible young men. She could expect to marry well and to lead an elegant, comfortable life. But, for Florence, that wasn't enough. She already knew that she wanted to do something really important with her life. She longed, she later said, "for something worth doing instead of frittering time away on useless trifles."

She was not alone in her frustration. Women of her class were hobbled by society's rules about how they should spend their days, what they should care about, who could be their friends. There were books they weren't supposed to read, places they weren't supposed to go, even thoughts they weren't supposed

William Nightingale with one of his wife's four sisters. Much as Florence's father loved his clever younger daughter, he also loved tranquility. When Florence was at odds with her mother and sister, he rarely took her side. This sketch is by Hilary Bonham Carter, one of Florence's cousins.

to think. The feelings and ambitions they bottled up were bound to burst out somehow. The result was a strange fashion for "delicacy." Many women prided themselves on their oversensitive natures. They greeted trivial events with weeping, shrieking, or fainting; their maids carried bottles of "smelling salts" – a sharp-smelling ammonia mixture – to revive them when they swooned.

More serious disappointments might send them to bed for weeks, months, or even years, with vague complaints such as weakness, dizziness, or palpitations (a pounding heart).

An artistic style called Romanticism encouraged this behavior. Romantic novels told breathtaking tales of passion and tragedy; Romantic poems celebrated loss and death rather than success and happiness; Romantic paintings featured looming cliffs, stunted trees, or storm-tossed shipwrecks. Imagine a demure young woman sitting in a sunny parlor and reading *The Mysteries of Udolpho*, one of the most popular novels of the time:

> The belief of [Montoni's] death gave [Emily's] spirits a sudden shock, and she grew faint as she saw him in imagination, expiring at her feet.
>
> "They are coming!" cried Madame Montoni. "I hear their steps – they are at the door!"
>
> Emily turned her languid eyes to the door, but terror deprived her of utterance. The key sounded in the lock; the door opened, and Montoni appeared, followed by three ruffian-like men. "Execute your orders," said he, turning to them, and pointing to his wife, who shrieked, but was immediately carried from the room; while Emily sunk, senseless, on a couch. . . .

Emotion was everything. Drama was everything. When frailty and hysteria were seen as the marks of a true lady, how many women would boast about their sturdy good health and unshakable calm?

Although Florence was highly intelligent and energetic, and capable of iron self-discipline, she grew up with this notion of delicacy, and it affected her reactions to life. She became violently upset over minor setbacks. When people opposed her, even on the most reasonable grounds, she reviled them as enemies and traitors. In later years she spoke constantly of her feeble health, and often predicted that she would die young.

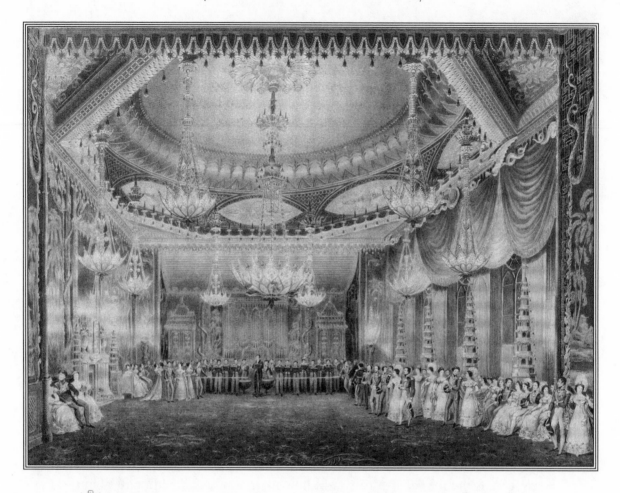

The pleasures of a dance, around 1820. Proper young couples could not go off alone for an evening; instead, they flirted and romanced at entertainments like this dance at the Brighton Pavilion. The pavilion was one of the extravagances built by the Prince of Wales (Prinny) before George III died.

As the Industrial Revolution brought factories and pollution to Britain's land-scape, it also brought strong currents of religious and social conscience. Many people were deeply troubled by the poverty and misery of workers who slaved indoors for long hours and went home to filthy, disease-filled slums. Also, the French Revolution of 1789–99 had reminded the wealthy that, if the poor were too badly treated, they might overthrow society altogether – and perhaps chop off some heads in the process.

In 1825 trade unions were made legal, so laborers could reject cruel or dangerous working conditions. In 1833 slavery was banned throughout the British Empire. In 1843 a Factory Act was passed, limiting child labor and requiring children to attend school. In 1848 a Board of Health was established, to take the first small steps in cleaning up the contagion of the slums. Religious movements like Reformism and Evangelicalism preached against idle extravagance, and insisted that going to church on Sunday wasn't enough to save one's soul. Instead, salvation must be found through a lifetime of piety, hard work, noble principles, and good deeds – the "something worth doing" that Florence longed for.

On February 7, 1837 – not long before Florence's seventeenth birthday – something happened that would change her life. "God spoke to me," she wrote, "and called me to His service." This heavenly summons reassured her, and filled her with faith and a sense of peace. She was no longer a misfit, a troublesome girl rebelling against her place in life. If she was different from other people, it was because she was special. She had a divine mission. She had been chosen by God to be His instrument.

What exactly did God want Florence to do? He didn't say.

Florence would have to work that out for herself.

A few months later, another well-born young Englishwoman was called to service. In the last few years of George III's life, the line of royal succession had been in doubt. George's son and heir, the Prince of Wales (scornfully called Prinny), was a spoiled, vain spendthrift. Prinny's only child had died childless

George III had been a weak, unwise king with a disease that gave him fits of madness, and his son Prinny had lurched from scandal to scandal, so the monarchy had lost much of its popularity. The young Queen Victoria soon married an admirably intelligent, sensible German prince named Albert, and started a family (she would have nine children). Victoria and Albert set an example of respectability, honor, and duty that restored the royal family's good name.

in 1817, and Prinny's wife had deserted him, so the next heir would have to come from one of Prinny's middle-aged brothers. There were a couple of hasty marriages, and one of the brothers managed to sire a daughter. She was born in May 1819 (almost exactly one year before Florence) and named Victoria.

Prinny ruled (as George IV) for ten years after his father died, and his brother William IV ruled for the next seven. On William's death in 1837, the throne of Great Britain and all her dominions passed to Victoria. She was eighteen years old. She would be queen – and later empress – until she died in the next century, at the age of eighty-one.

CHAPTER THREE

WORSE THAN DUST AND NOTHING

Why, as a child in the nursery, when her sister had shown a healthy plea-sure in tearing her dolls to pieces, had she shown an almost morbid one in sewing them up again? Why was she driven now to minister to the poor in cottages, to watch by sick-beds, to put her dog's wounded paw into elaborate splints as if it was a human being?

— Lytton Strachey, 1918

N VICTORIAN TIMES, UPPER-CLASS GIRLS WERE EXPECTED TO grow up not over years, but almost overnight. One day you were a child; then your parents decided that your childhood was over, and you put up your long hair, set aside your games, and "came out" of childhood into the grown-up world. You went to tea parties, formal dinners, and balls, and pursued a young lady's most urgent mission: the acquisition of a suitable husband.

Both Nightingale sisters were to come out in the summer of 1839. It would be an expensive business. The family would have to host parties and dances, and invite dozens of young men and women. Then Flo and Parthe would be invited to lots of other people's balls, and they would meet as many potential husbands as possible. The high point of the season would be the girls' presentation at court, when they were formally introduced to Queen Victoria.

But of course, declared Fanny, Embley was far too small for all that entertaining. It would need six more bedrooms, a new kitchen, and a complete remodeling and redecorating. While the work was being done, the family would make another tour of Europe.

They set out in September 1837, in a large carriage (designed by the versatile William Nightingale) drawn by three pairs of horses. They took along half a dozen servants. For a year and a half they traveled, crossing France, spending time in Italy, going on to Switzerland. Florence whiled away the long hours in the carriage by gazing at the romantic landscapes of Europe and dreaming up thrilling adventures with herself (of course) as heroine. In the cities, they visited historic sites, attended parties and concerts, and met prominent people. With her quick wit and fluent French, Florence was much admired. She discovered that she adored dancing and music, especially opera. And travel was so thrilling! It seemed that this difficult daughter was finally turning into the amusing, elegant lady that Fanny wanted her to be.

The lands they visited were very different from today's European countries, which have been shaped (and are still being shaped) by wars and revolutions. There were more countries, and far more kings and queens presiding over royal courts. The political balance shifted constantly, with alliances being made and broken as rulers schemed to extend their power. With so much tension, flashes of violence were inevitable.

Traveling through this unrest, Florence was exploring history and politics in real life. Italy was not yet united into a single country, and after the defeat of Napoleon's armies some regions of Italy had been given to Austria. Italian patriots were demanding Italy's independence. As the Austrian government tried to crush the rebellion, Italian scientists and scholars escaped to Switzerland. In Geneva, Florence met people who had been persecuted, even tortured, for their passionate political beliefs.

Suddenly, danger came too close. France and Switzerland were on the brink of war, and the Swiss were preparing to defend themselves. The Swiss army commandeered all the horses in Geneva, leaving the Nightingales' splendid carriage sitting useless. While Fanny and the girls huddled indoors, William scrambled to find replacement horses, and the family hastily set off for Paris. The crisis in Geneva was soon over, but the experience burned a hole in Florence's heart. While most people she knew wasted their lives chatting and partying, these patriots were doing great things. They were shaping the world to come.

Sharp-tongued, intellectual Mary Clarke would remain Florence's close friend for the rest of her life. In 1847 Clarkey married Julius Mohl, a scholar who was also a devoted friend to Florence. The sketch is by Hilary Bonham Carter.

But once the family reached Paris, Florence forgot her guilt. She was caught up again in the dizzying whirl of society. The Nightingales met Mary Clarke, or "Clarkey," a lively, fascinating hostess whose dinner parties attracted the most brilliant men in Paris. Clarkey was famous for saying what she thought, even if it was tactless or rude. Like Florence, she was exasperated by women who wouldn't make use of their brains. "Why don't they talk about interesting things?" she demanded. "I can't abide them in my drawing room." She approved of the Nightingale sisters, though. She introduced them to famous authors and artists, and helped them find their way through fashionable Paris.

Even in the midst of this excitement and glamor, Florence found time for studying. She kept careful notes about what she saw, and what she learned about local laws and living conditions. She made up a table of the exact distances they traveled, and their departure and arrival times. In another table she listed all the operas she went to, recording her opinion of the music, words, and singing. Throughout her life she would keep copious notes on her thoughts and observations, on whatever scraps of paper came to hand. Her passion for precise facts and numbers would prove to be one of her greatest gifts.

⚜

In April 1839 the family arrived home in England, and went to London for an interlude of glittering balls, late-night suppers, handsome dance partners, and, of course, presentation to the new queen. But all of this was soon over, and Florence found herself back in the trivial, frustrating routine she so despised – a life that Clarkey (tactless as ever) dismissed as "faddling twaddling and the endless tweedling of nosegays in jugs." Even her beloved father bored her. He insisted on reading the newspaper aloud to his daughters, a torture that Florence compared to "lying on one's back, with one's hands tied, and having liquid poured down one's throat."

The Nightingales had visits from interesting statesmen and scholars. They were much involved with the Palmerston family, who lived nearby; Lord Palmerston, an impulsive, reform-minded politician, was the government's

Mai Smith – the sister of Florence's father, and the mother of Shore Smith – was a kind, patient woman who made many efforts, over the years, to help and defend Florence. She kept trying to persuade Fanny that Florence was not like other young women: "I don't think you have any idea of half that is in her," she insisted. In later years, Mai's husband, Sam – Fanny's brother – often helped Florence with business matters.

foreign minister. Florence was close friends with two of her nearby cousins, Hilary Bonham Carter and Marianne Nicholson. But when there was company, Florence complained that she had no time for serious thought; when the family was alone, she was bored and irritable. Aunt Mai understood her despair, and tried – not very successfully – to convince Fanny that her daughter needed intelligent work. Clarkey suggested, in a letter, that she try writing as an occupation, but Florence retorted that "writing is only a substitute for living." She felt useless and wasted, guilty for the luxuries she had enjoyed in Europe, and deeply troubled by the misery of the poor. People were starving,

One of the duties of a country lady was to visit worthy laborers when they were ill, taking them small comforts – perhaps a cozy shawl and a flask of broth – and reading them a few passages from the Bible or some other spiritually uplifting book.

grinding their lives away in grim labor, dying of horrible sicknesses. "All the people I see are eaten up with care or poverty or disease," she wrote. She fretted so much that she made herself sick. She began daydreaming more than ever – even in the middle of dinner parties – and she felt guilty about that too.

God had called on her once to serve Him. Why had He never spoken to her again? Had He changed his mind? Had He decided that she was unworthy after all?

❧

Whenever possible, Florence made herself useful by caring for sick relatives. She found great satisfaction in easing their misery by bringing hot or cold compresses, ordering special dishes – clear soups, meat jellies, and egg puddings – to tempt their weak appetites, reading to them, or simply sitting by the bedside and offering solace. In 1843, when the sister of one of her friends died in childbirth, she went to help with the motherless infant. Early in 1845 she spent a month caring for Shore Smith when he was getting over a bad case of measles. Later that year she nursed her grandmother through a serious illness, and then turned her attentions to Mrs. Gale, the old nurse who

---

THE ETIQUETTE OF DEATH

Death was a familiar visitor in Victorian homes. Most people died at home, and that was where their bodies were laid out (prepared for burial). As a result, the Victorians came to terms with their grief by celebrating it. Women wore special mourning costumes after a death; the exact costume, and the number of months it was worn, depended on the relationship to the deceased. There was even special mourning jewelry, made of jet (polished coal) or ebony (black wood). Strands of hair from dead relatives were woven into flower patterns and used in jewelry – or in full-sized wreaths to decorate the parlor, next to black-framed photographs of babies who had died at birth. Now that death so often happens in hospitals, and is treated with whispers and embarrassment, these rites may seem bizarre to us – but they helped people deal with loss, and that was what mattered.

had cared for Parthe and Flo when they were small. Mrs. Gale died holding Florence's hand.

She also went to the cottages of poor people who needed help, taking them food, clothes, medicine, whatever Fanny would let her have. She assisted at difficult births and kept a vigil at deathbeds. It pleased her that she could comfort people, but there was so little she could do for them; wasn't there some better way to use her intelligence and energy? And her kind acts exasperated her mother. Why would a marriageable young woman throw away her time in a sickroom? How would that ever win her a husband? Besides, what would people say?

Despite Fanny's alarm, Florence did attract suitors. Marianne Nicholson's brother Henry fell in love with her and hoped to marry her. She stalled for six years, perhaps keeping him around because she was so fond of his sister. When she finally turned Henry down in the spring of 1845, he was brokenhearted, and Marianne was so angry at the way her brother had been treated that she ended their friendship. Five years later, poor Henry was dead, drowned while traveling in Spain.

Richard Monckton Milnes also wanted to marry her. Milnes was brilliant and charming

Richard Monckton Milnes was celebrated as a generous host and a generous man. The novelist William Thackeray said he "always put you in a good humour with yourself." The author and critic Thomas Carlyle joked that if Christ came to earth again, "Monckton Milnes would ask him to breakfast." Florence admired him too. "He treated all his fellow mortals as if they were his brothers and sisters," she said. But in the end she refused to marry him.

and wealthy. He knew everybody and he had been everywhere. He was a Member of Parliament and had a strong social conscience, caring especially about the welfare of children. Florence apparently came to love him, and in many ways they seemed ideally suited. But although she enjoyed seeing him and sharing his gilded life, she always came home to her own nagging conscience. With so many people suffering in the world, she was desperate to do something useful. But what?

Where did people get help when they were ill? If they could afford it, they might consult a physician. Physicians had been exploring human anatomy for centuries, and they could prescribe drugs (physic) and procedures that had worked in the past. But much of their medicine was based on superstition, or on association; for example, a spotted plant would be used against a disease that caused spots. Other cures went back to ancient Greek and Roman times. Many problems were blamed on excessive blood, so it was common practice to cut open a patient's vein and drain off a few bowls of blood – sometimes so much that the patient fainted. (Blood could also be removed by sticking dozens of leeches – blood-sucking slugs – to the patient's body.) There were all kinds of medical theories – complicated by religious and philosophical musings on what life was, and where (or Whom) it came from – but there was not enough open-minded, systematic research.

Student physicians got most of their training by reading books and helping in hospitals. Because they wanted to be thought of as gentlemen, they generally avoided handling patients, or doing anything that might be considered physical work.

Someone who had an injury, or needed something removed, might see a surgeon. Surgeons were less exalted than physicians – surgery had begun as a sideline of barbering – so they would do hands-on work like sewing up wounds and setting broken bones, and even cutting out diseased organs. Most of them had learned their trade as apprentices (assistants) of experienced surgeons.

The laboratory of a chemist-druggist's shop in the 1840s. Apothecaries were lower on the social scale than physicians and surgeons. They were originally paid to dispense drugs, but they often traveled to patients' homes and gave medical advice, especially if people couldn't afford a physician. Gradually, many apothecaries turned into what we call family doctors, or general practitioners (GPs). Others remained in the "physic" business as chemist-druggists, preparing medications and selling them in their shops.

Very few people went to hospital at that time, partly because those who went in often didn't come out again. If you did end up in hospital, you would be cared for by physicians and their students. There were women called nurses, but they weren't trained in medical procedures. If you were lucky, they gave you some of the care your family would have given you at home – keeping you fed and somewhat clean, and changing the dressings on your wounds. By one description, a nurse was "a coarse old woman, always ignorant, usually dirty, often brutal . . . in bunched-up sordid garments. . . ." Because they were doing a miserable job for very little pay, many nurses drank as they worked. Some earned extra money as prostitutes. This was a vicious circle: as long as nurses were seen as indecent drunks, few self-respecting women would work at the job.

The exception to this was the nursing sisterhoods. Some Catholic and Anglican nuns, and some women of other religions, chose to serve God by going into the hospitals and caring for the suffering. Their powers were very limited; physicians were in charge of everything, and many of them scoffed at these women and their common sense. Still, the nursing sisters' experience, dedication, and kindness made them indispensable. Because the work was physically unpleasant, and the risk of catching a disease was high, there was always a shortage of nursing sisters.

By the summer of 1844, when she was twenty-four, Florence was sure that her destiny lay in helping the sick. She asked an American visitor, a famous social reformer, if he thought it would be "unsuitable and unbecoming . . . to devote herself to works of charity in hospitals and elsewhere as Catholic sisters do?" He admitted that it would be unconventional, but he encouraged her all the same: "If you have a vocation for that way of life, act up to your inspiration." He assured her that there was nothing unladylike about dedicating herself to helping others.

But by 1845, she had done enough nursing to realize that the job required more than kindness and good intentions. If she really wanted to help, she needed practical knowledge. She needed to learn as much about nursing as she possibly could. But how?

The chief physician at the infirmary (hospital) in nearby Salisbury was a family friend. Florence resolved that she would persuade him to let her spend

EVIL SPIRITS AND MIASMAS

Everybody knew that people got sick in hospitals. Everybody knew that wounds and surgical incisions could become horribly – even fatally – infected. But nobody could agree on where disease and infection came from. Some people believed that a miasma, or dangerous gas, sprang up in filthy places like sewers and garbage dumps. Some thought infections came from a flaw in the patient. Some blamed evil spirits or said piously that it was all God's will, and some insisted that infections just happened all by themselves.

There were people who realized that infections were being passed from person to person, but they couldn't explain how this happened. Were disease seeds scattered by the wind, like dandelion seeds? Did clouds of tiny disease insects flutter through the air? Since they couldn't explain how infections were spread, nothing was done to prevent them. Hospital patients with different diseases were jammed in together, bedded down in sheets still soiled by earlier occupants, and blood-sucking parasites like fleas and lice carried illness from bed to bed. Surgeons' instruments were filthy, and if their coats were stiff with dried blood, that just showed how much experience they had. Almost anything that could be done in the stench and gore of a hospital could be done better, and far more safely, in a clean home.

three months at the hospital. She would study nursing as methodically as she had studied everything else, and she would turn herself into a first-class, expert nurse.

She proposed this exciting idea to her family – and they exploded. Fanny was outraged, alternating between fits of weeping and attacks of cruel accusations.

Parthe was appalled. Hospitals were not only disgusting but dangerous. They held horrors not fit for a lady's eyes, let alone her dainty hands. Worse yet, there were all kinds of scandalous stories about what went on between surgeons and nurses. The whole idea was absolutely out of the question.

Even her father was disgusted. After all that education, all that culture, how could Florence be so spoiled and ungrateful?

Florence was beside herself with despair. She had finally found the answer, and now it was denied her. "I shall never do anything, and am worse than dust and nothing," she wrote in a woeful letter to Hilary Bonham Carter. "Oh for some strong thing to sweep this loathsome life into the past." In a note to herself, she scribbled, "I cannot live – forgive me, oh Lord, and let me die, this day let me die." There was nothing, *nothing*, worth living for.

CHAPTER FOUR

BIRD IN A GILDED CAGE

Resignation! I never understood that word!
— Florence Nightingale

HEN HER PLAN TO STUDY NURSING IN THE SALISBURY HOSPITAL was rejected by her family, Florence seemed to retreat into the life of a country lady. She cared for the sick whenever she was needed. She went to dinner parties, balls, and other social gatherings. But she spent most of her days on tedious, trivial duties. She sorted out the towels and bedding in the linen room. She made lists of the china and glassware. She supervised the servants' jam-making. But what was the point of all this counting and organizing? Why couldn't she learn something useful? Once, looking back on her achievements over the previous two weeks, she calculated that she had done some reading and "learnt seven tunes by heart. Written various letters. Ridden with Papa. Paid eight visits. Done Company. And that is all."

At night, though, she lived a secret life. She was determined not to give up her dreams. If she couldn't go to Salisbury to become a nurse, she would teach herself to be much, much more. Night after night, she studied, huddled in a shawl and working by candlelight. She read official reports about public

LADIES OF LETTERS

Before cars and telephones, letter-writing was a vital part of a lady's life. Just arranging lunch with a friend might take three or four handwritten notes back and forth. Mail was picked up and delivered several times a day, and a note sent in the morning might well be answered by evening. At first the mail was carried by fast horse-drawn coaches, but by the mid-1800s trains were taking over the job. Soon after that, urgent messages could be sent by telegraph; the hustle of the modern world was taking over.

health and sanitary arrangements in Britain. She got friends to send her information on European sanitation and mortality (death rates), so that she could compare statistics. Chart upon chart, notebook upon notebook, she built up an impressive knowledge of sanitation and sickness.

One of her helpful friends was the Chevalier Bunsen, a German aristocrat who was a close friend of Queen Victoria and Prince Albert's. When Florence was twenty-six, Bunsen sent her the yearbook of the Institution of Deaconesses, in Kaiserswerth, near Düsseldorf, Germany. This was a combined teachers' college, prison, orphanage, and hospital where respectable women could learn nursing skills from physicians, under the watchful eye of a clergyman. The school was strictly run and utterly respectable, and it sounded like the answer to Florence's prayers. "There my heart is," she wrote, "and there, I trust, will one day be my body." How could her parents object to such an irreproachable institute?

After all the fuss they had made last time, though, she was reluctant to raise the issue. By night she pursued her secret studies, and by day she continued her household tasks and fashionable entertainments. She was still seeing

MICROCOSM dedicated to the London Water Companies · BROUGHT FORTH ALL MONSTROUS, ALL PRODIGIOUS THINGS, HYDRAS, AND GORGONS, AND CHIMERAS DIRE. Vide Milton

MONSTER SOUP commonly called THAMES WATER, being a correct representation of that precious stuff doled out to us!

A cartoon from the early 1800s, mocking the pollution of London's great river, the Thames. Because sewage was handled carelessly, drinking water was often fouled by human and industrial waste. But while people complained that the water's smell gave them headaches and nausea, most didn't believe they could die from a "bug" too small to see.

Richard Monckton Milnes, and still – to her mother's exasperation – putting off the question of marriage. Despite her labors at night, she remained deeply ashamed of her "vanity, love of display, love of glory." She blamed herself for not leading a simpler life, not having a purer heart, and tormented herself with accusations. No wonder God didn't want her, she anguished; she wasn't good enough for Him. She fretted herself sick, and daydreamed constantly. Often she imagined herself as Mrs. Monckton Milnes, enacting splendid reforms with the support of her wealthy, powerful husband.

In the fall of 1847, Florence was so ill and miserable that she took to her bed. Hoping to cheer her up, an older couple who were close friends – Charles and Selina Bracebridge – invited her to spend the winter in Rome. Florence went, and she was thrilled by the trip. She spent many hours touring galleries and churches. She passed a whole afternoon in the Sistine Chapel, enraptured by Michelangelo's famous paintings of biblical subjects on the chapel's ceiling. "Oh how happy I was!" she wrote later. The gorgeous holy paintings filled her with inspiration and renewed her religious faith. With all the excitement, she soon felt well again, and before long she was back on the dance floor.

While she was in Rome, Florence became friends with Sidney Herbert and his new wife, Elizabeth. Herbert was a brilliant, handsome man, owner of vast estates, son and heir of the Earl of Pembroke, but the couple were modest and devout, and dedicated to works of charity. They were especially interested in hospital reform, and were in the midst of building a home for invalids. They must have been astonished to discover that elegant Miss Nightingale knew so much about the subject.

When they all returned to England, the Herberts introduced Florence to other influential people who cared about improving the hospital system, and she became known as something of an expert on public health. The Herberts approved of her plan to go to Kaiserswerth, and the Chevalier Bunsen was planning to send his own daughter there. How much more respectable could a school be? Yet Florence still didn't raise the subject with her family.

In the fall of 1848, it suddenly seemed that God was smiling on her. Parthe had been unwell, and was going to a spa in Germany to recover her health.

Poor families line up at a public pump to collect water for washing and drinking. During a cholera epidemic in 1854, a London doctor, John Snow, marked the deaths on a map and showed that many of the victims had drunk from the same pump. He had the pump handle removed, and the number of deaths dropped. His detective work proved that poisonous water was no joke, and by 1875 London had a new water and sewage system.

The rest of the family would go as far as Frankfurt. Frankfurt was close to Kaiserswerth; surely Florence could manage to visit the institute for a week or two. It was exactly the chance she had been waiting for.

The tantalizing opportunity was soon snatched away. There was political unrest in Frankfurt, so the family stayed in England after all. Florence was shattered, convinced that God had stepped in to keep her from her goal. He still found her unworthy. "My God what am I to do," she agonized to herself. "I cannot go on any longer. . . ."

By the spring of 1849, when the Nightingales went to London for the social season, Florence was in a sorry state. Her mind was always wandering; she stumbled through the days, often with little idea of what was going on around her. In the past she had wondered what a life of laziness and emptiness would do to her mind. "I see so many of my kind who have gone mad for want of something to do," she had written, just the year before. Now she feared that she truly was going insane.

In the midst of her wretchedness, Richard Monckton Milnes announced that he could not wait any longer. Once and for all, would she marry him or would she not?

What was Florence to do? She longed to pursue her dreams, to be a great benefactor and heroine, yet her plans seemed doomed to failure. She cared deeply for Richard – "the man I adored," she later called him – and dreaded losing him. But as his wife and hostess, as the mother of his children, would she ever have the time and freedom to follow her own calling? Should she give up love and cling to her dream? Or abandon it as hopeless, and settle for marriage and motherhood?

She turned him down, but she could barely explain her reasons to herself. She wrote pages of painful justifications, trying to make sense of her decision. And no one could explain it to her mother. What a brilliant marriage it would have been! What a dazzling son-in-law had been thrown away! Fanny was more determined than ever that her stubborn, rebellious daughter must never get her own way.

Missing her dear friend and suitor, and scorned by most of her family, Florence sank into despondency. She was plagued by headaches and a hacking cough. Her mind was still going blank, and sometimes she fainted. Once

THE ANGEL IN THE HOUSE

Florence Nightingale had good reason to be wary of marriage. In Victorian times a married woman was supposed to be a paragon of virtue: high-minded, self-sacrificing, devoted to her husband and family, "the angel of the house." But that "angel" was decidedly short on legal rights. She could not open a bank account or own property or write a will. She could not divorce her husband, and if he divorced her she would almost certainly lose her children. Her husband's duty was to judge right from wrong, and direct his family accordingly; her duty was to trust and follow him. The poet Tennyson summed up their roles:

Man with the head, and woman with the heart;
Man to command, and woman to obey.

again the Bracebridges came to the rescue. They were planning to visit Egypt, Greece, and other European countries, and they persuaded Fanny to let Florence go with them. This time, though, the pleasures of travel could not distract her from her brooding. As she pondered the animal-headed gods of ancient Egypt, and the jealous, all-too-human gods of ancient Greece, she struggled with her own demanding God. What did He want? What was she supposed to do? Many of the notes in her diary describe her poor health and her conversations with God. On her birthday in 1850, she wrote, "May 12: To-day I am 30 – the age Christ began his mission. Now no more childish things. No more love. No more marriage. Now Lord let me think only of Thy Will, what Thou willest me to do. Oh Lord Thy Will, Thy Will."

In June she wrote that she was "physically and morally ill and broken down, a slave." By July 1 she "lay in bed and called on God to save me." Alarmed

by her decline, and fearing that she was losing her mind, the Bracebridges made a bold decision. They took Florence to Berlin, and from there – at last – to Kaiserswerth.

Florence stayed at the Institute of Deaconesses for two weeks, not studying, but helping out and talking to the staff. By the end of the visit, her mood and her health had improved dramatically. But then the travelers had to go home.

After the first few hours of welcome, Florence seemed to be right back where she had started. Fanny had somehow learned about the visit to Kaiserswerth, and she was furious. Her husband refused to stand up for his difficult daughter. There was no question of her returning to the institute, they declared; a young lady's place was at home, and home was where this young lady would stay.

The most hysterical opposition came from her sister. Less gifted, less attractive, and entirely lacking Florence's energy and determination, Parthe could only coast in her sister's shadow. Most women married young in those days; now that Parthe was over thirty and still single, it seemed unlikely that she would ever find a husband. As long as Florence was at home, Parthe enjoyed a small share of her popularity. If Florence went away, Parthe would be nobody.

Both parents blamed Florence's absence for her sister's ill health and hysteria, and insisted that Florence spend the next six months in virtual slavery to Parthe. Florence – consumed by guilt, as always – agreed. For half a year the sisters sang together, sketched together, walked and talked together. Parthe improved, but Florence was plunged back into dreaming and despair. In

An engraving of Florence, around 1850, based on a drawing by Parthe. Beside her is Athena, an owl she brought back from Greece. Athena was her dear pet for five years.

January 1851 she lamented, "In my thirty-first year I see nothing desirable but death. . . ."

❦

But now that she had seen Kaiserswerth, had stood in its grounds and breathed its air, it was no longer a distant dream. It was real, it was her destiny, and she *would* go back. In June 1851 – with her slavery to Parthe over, and with Richard Monckton Milnes engaged to someone else – she told her family that she was returning to Kaiserswerth, and she would not be refused.

When Fanny realized that she couldn't prevent the trip, she contrived to make it as humiliating as possible. Parthe was ill again – all Florence's fault, said Fanny – so mother and daughters would go to Germany together. Florence could then sneak off to Kaiserswerth, but she must not write to any of her friends from there, or tell anyone where she had gone.

❦

However much Florence had wanted to work at the institute, she must have been taken aback by the living conditions she endured once she got there. Students rose at five in the morning, worked long hours, and were allowed ten-minute breaks for skimpy meals of bread, soup, and vegetables. Worse yet, she was disappointed by the poor training and hygiene – perhaps because she had already learned so much on her own. Still, she was finally working in her chosen field. She made painstaking records of how the hospital was organized. She paid special attention to the way the superintendent managed the staff and their day-to-day procedures. This woman "has to consider herself as the mother of the house," she noted. Florence also shared the grimmest chores of the hospital, assisting physicians and surgeons as they did their job.

❦

That job was changing dramatically. In 1832 Britain's Anatomy Act had made it easier for doctors to acquire unclaimed corpses, so they could dissect them and see how various diseases affected the body. Also, better tools were being invented, and research was becoming more scientific. One way and another, doctors were getting a clearer idea of how the human body worked, and exactly what went wrong with it. They could focus on diagnosing the problem, instead of just treating the symptoms.

Many of the new medical tools of that time are still in use today. In the 1820s an early version of the stethoscope let doctors hear the distinctive noises of the healthy or unhealthy heart, lungs, and other organs. The microscope was drastically improved, so they could study body tissues and fluids. Thermometers had been around for a long time, but after 1840 the meaning

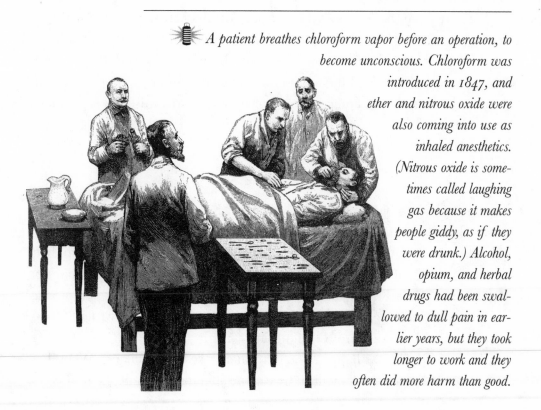

A patient breathes chloroform vapor before an operation, to become unconscious. Chloroform was introduced in 1847, and ether and nitrous oxide were also coming into use as inhaled anesthetics. (Nitrous oxide is sometimes called laughing gas because it makes people giddy, as if they were drunk.) Alcohol, opium, and herbal drugs had been swallowed to dull pain in earlier years, but they took longer to work and they often did more harm than good.

of a high or low temperature was better understood. Thermometers went from being a foot (30 cm) long and taking twenty minutes to produce a reading, to being half as long and four times as fast. A spirometer was developed, to measure breathing and test how well the lungs were working, and a sphygmograph recorded the speed and strength of the pulse, showing how well the heart was pumping blood. In 1851 the ophthalmoscope was invented, so doctors could peer inside the living eye.

As medical journals were published and experts from different countries put their heads together, the systems of the body – circulatory (blood), digestive, nervous, muscular, glandular, and so on – were gradually mapped, and the secrets of disease began to unfold.

Amid all these advances, there was one area where medicine was moving backwards. As long as treatment had been more or less unregulated, women had played a major role. But as doctors became officially trained and licensed, the female sex was left out in the cold. Women were "psychologically unfit for higher education," it was claimed. Too much brainwork would "divert energy from the womb and lead to sterility and hysteria." In any case the medical scene, with its suffering and gore and naked body parts, was seen as no place for a lady.

Fanny and Parthe would surely have agreed.

❧

Florence wrote to her mother and sister from Kaiserswerth, begging them to accept her thirst for knowledge. "Give me time, give me faith," she pleaded. "Trust me, help me." It was to no avail. Fanny and Parthe had made up their minds to be revolted and, despite his love of learning, her father would not defend her. When Florence rejoined her mother and sister, after completing her training and receiving high praise for her excellence, she wrote, "I was treated as if I had come from committing a crime."

Still, her family was happy enough to make use of her talents. When her father needed a month of medical treatments at a distant clinic, he refused to go unless Florence made the journey with him. She nursed Parthe through yet another nervous crisis. Trapped at home, she wrote a tragic novel called *Cassandra*, about a young woman frustrated by her pointless, captive life. When this heroine is finally killed by her own family, she welcomes death: "Free – free – oh! divine freedom . . . !"

※

Florence attended an amputation at Kaiserswerth and found it fascinating – "This is life," she declared. The invention of anesthetics had made operations less brutal and ghastly, but surgeons still didn't understand the need for cleanliness. Many patients survived their operations but died later because their wounds were infected.

It's hard to believe, these days, how blind the Victorians were to infection. In 1847 a physician in Vienna noticed a puzzling difference between two maternity wards. In a ward staffed by student doctors, 29 percent of the mothers died of infection. In a ward staffed by student midwives, only 3 percent died. Why? He realized that the student doctors were cutting up diseased corpses and then caring for new mothers, without bothering to wash their hands or clean their instruments in between.

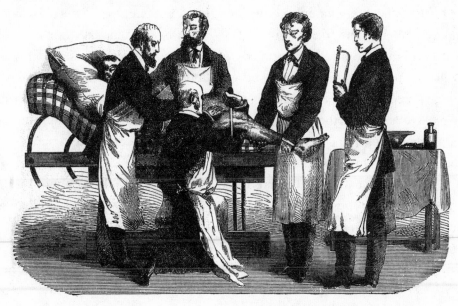

Desperate to continue her training, Florence arranged to work and study in Paris at a Catholic hospital run by an order of nuns, the Sisters of Charity. By this time, a number of friends and relatives – including Selina Bracebridge and Aunt Mai – were scolding Fanny for the way she treated Florence. Even Florence's father was beginning to think she should be allowed to go. While Fanny stalled, saying yes one day and no the next, Parthe complained of terrible pains; she declared that she was dying, and that it was Florence's fault. When Queen Victoria's personal physician said that Parthe was simply overindulged, and would be better away from her younger sister, Florence jumped on the excuse. She started packing for Paris.

She didn't get there; her great-aunt was ailing, and Florence was sent to nurse her. After the great-aunt died, Florence tried again to escape to the Sisters of Charity. This time she got to Paris, but was soon summoned home to help her grandmother through her final days.

And then, in the spring of 1853, the door to Florence's future suddenly swung open before her. A charity hospital for poor gentlewomen was being reorganized and moved to a new location. The hospital was run by two committees – one of men and one of women – and Liz Herbert suggested to a friend on the women's committee that Florence would make an ideal superintendent. The friend agreed. The Nightingales – needless to say – did not. Parthe ranted and Fanny raged. With his home turned into a war zone, William retreated to his club in London. But this time, for a change, he showed a little sympathy for his extraordinary daughter. While he would not openly take her side against the others, he did something even better: he granted her an allowance of £500 a year. (A middle-class family could live a simple but comfortable life on that amount.)

What came next was a bizarre twist. Marianne Nicholson thought it disgraceful that any cousin of hers should be a nurse. Besides, she was still angry that Florence hadn't married her poor brother Henry. She persuaded the committee to reject Florence. Fanny and Parthe were instantly furious; whatever *they* might say about Florence, how dare Marianne speak a word against her?

They hurled themselves into battle, and the committee appointed Florence after all. She would live at the hospital, and she would employ – at her own expense – a respectable older woman as housekeeper and chaperone.

While the committees were finding a suitable building and having it renovated, Florence saw one last chance to work with the Sisters of Charity. She hurried to Paris, started her training, and came down with measles. She had no choice but to give up yet again, and return home as soon as she was well enough to travel.

But not quite home – not this time. Back in England, she spurned her family and rented an apartment in London. Never again would her parents' house be her home.

SUPERINTENDENT NIGHTINGALE

"We are ducks," [Fanny Nightingale] said with tears in her eyes, "who have hatched a wild swan." But the poor lady was wrong; it was not a swan that they had hatched, it was an eagle.

– Lytton Strachey, 1918

N AUGUST 1853, AT THE AGE OF THIRTY-THREE, FLORENCE Nightingale started her first job. Her little hospital, just large enough for twenty-seven patients, would be at Number 1, Upper Harley Street. (Today Harley is the most famous medical street in the world, but at that time doctors were just beginning to open offices there.) Florence would not receive a salary – being paid wasn't ladylike – but she was promised full control of the institute and its finances.

Even as she lay in bed in Paris, sick with measles, she had been firing off letters to the committees. She had instructed them about furnishing the building. She had insisted that hot water be piped to every floor. She had ordered a dumbwaiter (like a small elevator) to carry meals from the kitchen up to the patients' rooms, pointing out that "without a system of this kind, the nurse is converted into a pair of legs." She had demanded a special call-bell system to summon the nurses when they were needed.

When she came back to London, though, almost nothing had been done. The committee members were arguing with each other, and the doctors were arguing with each other, and the money for alterations had been frittered away in waste and carelessness.

Florence soon fixed that. She made lists of all the items she had, and all the things she needed. She changed the inefficient shopping arrangements, buying supplies in large quantities to get discount prices. She restocked the kitchen and linen supplies, using anything she could get her hands on – turning Fanny's old curtains into bedcovers, for example. She drove out the hospital surgeon and replaced him with a more helpful one who would dispense drugs, saving money on druggist bills. She even had fifty-two pots of jam cooked up, to save on grocery bills. In short, her work was much like her housekeeping back at Embley, but on a somewhat larger scale.

Money was not her only concern. In her very first week, the committee announced that only Anglican patients would be admitted. Florence let the members know – in no uncertain terms – that women would be admitted regardless of their religion. Furthermore, she declared, their priests or rabbis or "muftis" (Muslim priests) would be allowed to visit them. And if the committee didn't agree, she would "wish them good morning" – in other words, resign – and that was that.

She got her way, but some of the committee members were aghast. They had expected a devoted, self-sacrificing saint in their house of healing – not this domineering bully poking her fingers into every pie. When her determination and force of character weren't enough to defeat the opposition, she fell back on schemes and stratagems. She manipulated committee members, playing them against one another – "and I always win," she boasted to her father.

No aspect of the hospital escaped her attention, and no problem was beyond her capabilities. At one point, with the hospital beds filling up and renovations still going on, she was coping with five dying patients, a gas leak, brawling laborers, and a drunken foreman. No matter; she sorted them all out.

While she arranged special comforts for those who were truly ill, she was no soft touch. She made short work of anyone who faked illness – such as the woman who left her own meals untouched but stole food from other patients' plates. A bedridden patient who was convinced that she couldn't eat "anything but Port Wine & cream" was soon "eating meat & taking long walks like other people." While Florence dealt with these and other cases, she kept notes on every imaginable topic, and condensed her conclusions into brisk, stern reports to the committees.

Within six months the institute was running efficiently, and Florence was having a wonderful time. Although Fanny still disapproved of her daughter's career, she sent the hospital generous gifts of fruit, flowers, vegetables, and game meats from the grounds of Embley. Despite all her work, Florence found time for dinners and parties, and moved among such prominent people as the poet Elizabeth Barrett Browning, and the authors George Eliot and Elizabeth Gaskell (who wrote under the name Mrs. Gaskell). She served tea to guests, using special china, in her private sitting-room. (Even Parthe tried to come and visit, but the effort was too much; she collapsed on the doorstep.) In January 1854, Florence wrote her father that "I begin the New Year with more true feeling of a happy New Year than I ever had in my life."

She spread happiness among her patients, too, caring for more than just their medical treatment. She worried about them, found money for them, arranged holidays for them before they returned to work. Their letters spoke of love and admiration: "How gratefully I accept your offer . . . ," "I cannot thank you enough . . . ," "You are our sunshine. . . ."

By spring, though, the hospital was in such good order that Florence was looking for a new challenge. Something had to be done about the nursing profession, with its low standards and bad reputation. Liz and Sidney Herbert were pushing for hospital reform – but without good nurses, how could there

Sidney Herbert had a magnificent country home in England, a house in the heart of fashionable London, and huge estates in Ireland and Scotland. He was secretary at war when Lord Palmerston was prime minister, and he later became Lord Herbert of Lea. Using friends like Herbert, Florence turned her personal resolve into political power.

be good hospitals? If only she could begin at the beginning, by hiring more suitable women and training them properly. But how?

She knew that King's College Hospital, in London, was being reorganized, so she turned to a surgeon friend who had a lot of influence there. If Florence could just get herself appointed Superintendent of Nurses, she could put a whole new system of nurse training in place. Fanny and Parthe heard of her plans, and it was time for the smelling salts again. Couldn't Florence do something respectable for a change? Open a penitentiary, perhaps?

These days, a registered nurse – a nurse who is fully qualified to work in a hospital – usually has four or five years of specialized university training. Nursing students study anatomy, chemistry, physiology, biology, and nutrition. They study microbiology, sociology, pharmacology, statistical analysis, and clinical ethics – among other things.

Think about what nurses can do today. They can give you pills, injections, and intravenous medications that a doctor has prescribed. They can keep track of your condition by using instruments such as the thermometer, stethoscope, and blood-pressure meter, by checking how you look and feel, and by asking strategic questions. They can take blood samples for testing or give you oxygen to breathe. If your breathing or your heart stops, they can use techniques to start it again.

And that's only standard nursing. Specialist nurses (in the operating room, the intensive-care unit, or the newborn unit, for example) have other skills for their particular duties.

In Florence Nightingale's day, hospital nurses could do almost none of these things. With the doctor's permission they could change dressings on wounds and dole out medicine, but that was about all. They were not medical professionals. They were more like servants – and usually not very good ones.

In the summer of 1854, a cholera epidemic swept through central London, and five hundred people died in the first ten days. Cholera causes vomiting, stomach cramps, and terrible diarrhea; victims can lose as much as four gallons (15 l) of body fluids a day. As the ill and dying flocked to overcrowded hospitals, many nurses caught the disease, and others fled for their lives. Since the areas hardest hit were the slums, a lot of the sick were street prostitutes, drunk and in rags. Florence set aside her dignity as a lady superintendent, and volunteered her services at a public hospital, undressing, washing, and nursing these pathetic patients.

Mrs. Gaskell admired Florence's courage and dedication, but noted that she could be strangely cold-hearted, even to the poor cottagers she had nursed in the past. "She has no friend – and she wants none," she said. "She stands perfectly alone, half-way between God and His creatures. . . . She will not go among the villagers now because her heart and soul are absorbed by her hospital plans, and as she says she can only attend to one thing at once."

⚜

While Florence schemed to start a nursing school, she was about to be swept up in world events. Two hundred years earlier, the vast Ottoman (Turkish) Empire had covered much of Europe, the Middle East, and northern Africa. As that empire slowly decayed, Russia had pushed westward, seeking more territory – including the valuable port of Constantinople, between the Black Sea and the Mediterranean. (Constantinople is now Istanbul, Turkey's major city.) The Turks had declared war on Russia in the fall of 1853. In March 1854, feeling threatened by Russian expansion, England and France also declared war on Russia.

Modern warfare is staggeringly expensive. Soldiers expect reasonable wages and living conditions, sophisticated equipment and effective medical care. A single tank or fighter jet can cost millions of dollars. Governments have to think hard before setting out on such a costly venture, no matter how strongly they may want to fight.

The picture was very different in Victorian Britain. Military ranks were still based on social class, as they had been for centuries. Senior officers bought their way into power, instead of earning their rank through painful experience. Some of them turned out to be military geniuses, but others were completely incompetent. As for the enlisted men, they were seen as cheap labor, like their brothers slaving in the mines and factories. When a government wanted to go to war, it was all too easy to send off thousands of these men, with whatever weapons and supplies came to hand.

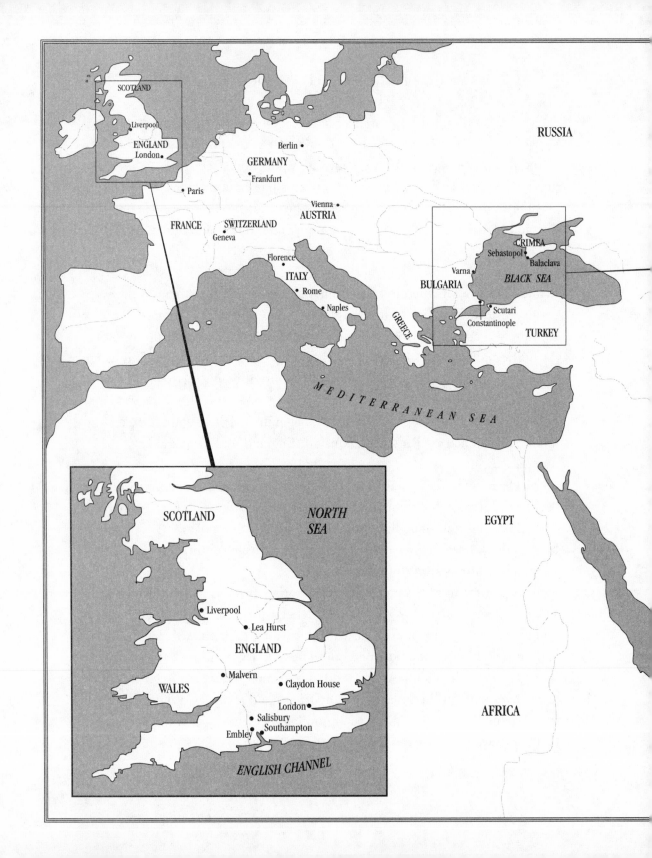

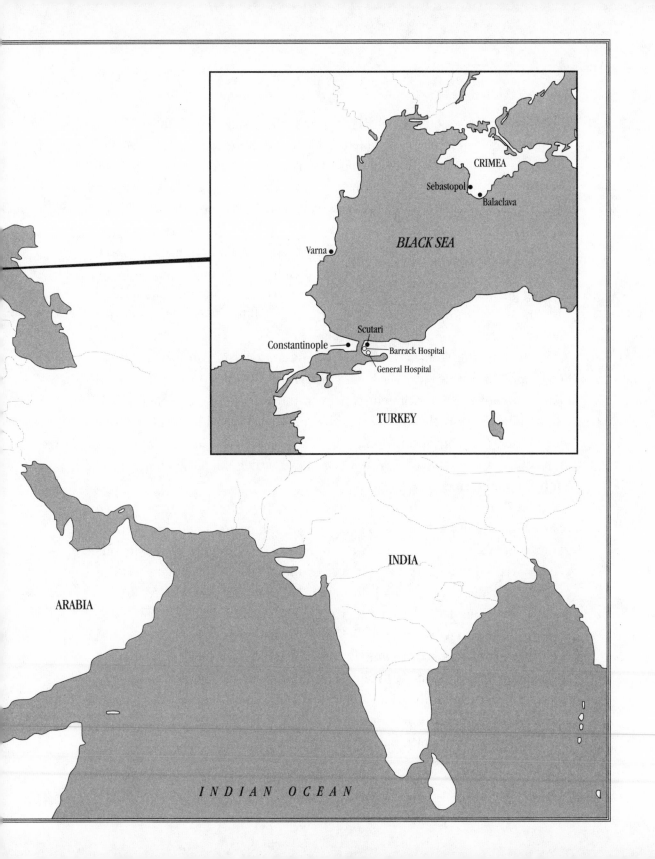

British troops set off for the Black Sea. At first they were sent to Varna, north of Constantinople. But cholera broke out among them, and instead of going into battle they were ordered to sail east to a peninsula called the Crimea. The main base of the Russian naval fleet in the Black Sea was in the port of Sebastopol. The Russians had a great fortress there, and the British and French allies hoped to seize it.

There weren't enough ships to carry the troops' equipment from Varna to the Crimea, so much of it had to be left behind – including tents, bedding, cooking gear, and medical supplies. Almost thirty thousand soldiers – some with cholera – were jammed into ships, and the bodies of those who died during the voyage were dumped into the sea.

By the time the French and British troops landed, some distance north of Sebastopol, they were sick, weak, and desperately short of food. A thousand men with cholera were shipped straight to the British base at Scutari, near Constantinople, and the rest began the march to Sebastopol. They came under heavy fire from the Russians, and thousands were killed or wounded; many others were dying of disease. Almost everything they needed had been left behind at Varna.

There were not enough carts to carry the victims – but then, there were no pack animals to draw the carts. There were no splints and bandages to tie up gashes and broken bones. There was no morphia to kill the pain. While surgeons sawed off mangled arms and legs by moonlight, their patients writhed and shrieked; there was no chloroform to make them unconscious. As soon as possible, the wounded – and another thousand cholera victims – were piled into ships and sent to Scutari.

A host of doctors accompanied the army, but the orderlies (male nurses) helping them were mostly unskilled. The British army did not use female nurses, partly because they had such a bad reputation, and partly because army doctors had no respect for their abilities. (The French soldiers were attended by the Sisters of Charity and had much better care.)

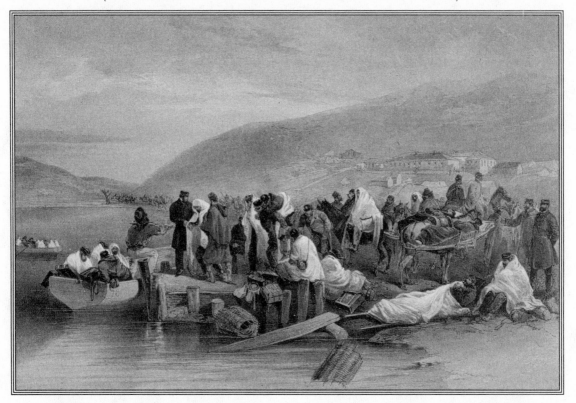

Sick and dying soldiers await transport out of Balaclava. Roger Fenton, a photographer in the Crimean War, described having cholera: after ninety minutes of vomiting, "cramp began in my legs and I had to be held upright and rubbed; in a short time it began in my arms and fingers, which began to turn blue. I could hardly breathe and felt my eyes staring very much." Fenton treated his diarrhea by drinking rice-water mixed with lime juice, and survived to document the war.

The Turks had given the British a hospital at Scutari, as well as a huge old barracks building. Since the hospital was nowhere near large enough for so many patients, army officials decided to turn the barracks into a second hospital. Improvements and equipment were ordered, but nothing was actually

Roger Fenton's photo of three privates in the Coldstream Guards. The engraving of the Battle of Inkerman shows the men wearing neat little mustaches, but in the cold of the Crimean winter many soldiers grew immense, wooly beards. After the war they took these beards home to England — often to the dismay of their wives and mothers.

done. The sick and wounded arrived at the Barrack Hospital to find no food; there was no kitchen. Men who were badly dehydrated by diarrhea could not get so much as a drink of water; there were no cups or buckets, and anyway there was no one to fetch the water. There were no beds, no chairs and tables – not even an operating table. There were no screens, so the most gruesome operations, the most agonizing deaths, took place in plain view. Lying on the filthy floor, wrapped in blankets that were stiff with blood and human waste, the patients were in an unspeakably pathetic state.

Word of these hellish conditions leaked back to Britain, through civilian observers and journalists. A scathing article in a London paper, *The Times*, told horrified families that their dear sons and husbands might wait "for a week, without the hand of a medical man coming near their wounds," and

In the days before machine-guns, before bombs and tanks and airplanes, war was imagined as a glorious adventure. Besides, the British still reveled in the memory of the great Battle of Waterloo, and the defeat of Emperor Napoleon. People cheered to see their gallant troops setting out for the Black Sea, dressed in bright red coats, and bearing swords and rifles with bayonets. But the reality of battles like the one at Inkerman (above) was brutal, and men who survived the enemy often lost their lives to disease.

that soldiers were dying as a result of "the medical staff of the British Army having forgotten that old rags are necessary for the dressing of wounds." *The Times* asked readers to send money to help the suffering soldiers, and donations poured in.

The government was in serious trouble. It had to correct this scandal, and quickly. The lost equipment must be replaced immediately. All necessary supplies must be sent out at once. And the army *must* have nurses.

The politician in charge of the army's finances happened to be Sidney Herbert. When he needed nurses, he knew exactly where to turn. He wrote a long, flattering letter to Florence, telling her that she was the only person in England who could assemble an official party of nurses and keep them in order once they reached Scutari. Not the least of her problems, he warned, would be "making the whole [nursing party] work smoothly with the medical and military authorities out there." It would all be very difficult. But would she take on the task?

In fact, Florence was already planning to go to Scutari at her own expense, with a few other nurses. Herbert's offer was even better. Not only would she have government support and financing, but the eyes of the country would be on her and her nurses. At last she could show the world how much they – and she – were capable of.

Within a day, it was agreed that Florence would lead the expedition. She would have the grand title of Superintendent of the Female Nursing Establishment of the English General Hospitals in Turkey. She would be fully in charge of forty nurses, but of course she would have to obey the army doctors in Scutari.

There was just one problem: where could she find forty acceptable nurses? The pay was not high, and the risk was considerable. Because the army didn't trust nurses and soldiers together, she could not hire any young women. For the same reason, the nurses would not be allowed outside the hospital except in groups, and any nurse who "misbehaved" would be sent home in disgrace.

At first, only fourteen experienced nurses could be found. Then the addition of twenty-four nursing sisters – fourteen Anglicans and ten Roman Catholics – brought the total up to thirty-eight. There was some concern about so many of the nurses being nuns. They might be more obedient to their Church superiors than to Florence. Also, she feared they might be more pious than practical; they might, she predicted, "flit about like angels without hands among the patients and soothe their souls while they leave their bodies dirty and neglected." But there was no way around it.

The nursing sisters would wear their nuns' habits. For the other nurses, a uniform had to be hastily designed and sewn: an ugly, ill-fitting gray dress and jacket, a short cloak, a brown sash with "Scutari Hospital" embroidered in red, and a plain white cap. One nurse complained bitterly to Florence, saying she would never have come if she'd known about the cap: "There are some things, Ma'am, one can't submit to."

In the midst of all this life-and-death urgency, Florence – now thirty-four years old, and officially appointed by Her Majesty's Government – felt obliged to seek her parents' permission to go to Scutari. For once, there was no resistance. Fanny and Parthe were thrilled by their connection to fame and glory. They wrote smugly to their friends and family, as if they had always known this day would come.

As for the shortage of supplies at Scutari, Sidney Herbert told Florence that he doubted things were as bad as they were reported. Mountains of material had been sent out – fifteen thousand sets of sheets, for example. They must all be there somewhere. In any case, he promised, the hospitals would be overflowing with goods by the time she arrived.

❧

On October 21, 1854 – just six days after Sidney Herbert asked her to take on the mission – Florence set off for Turkey. With her went thirty-eight nurses, her faithful friends the Bracebridges, and a few others.

A letter also went with her. It was from Richard Monckton Milnes. "You can undertake that," he wrote wistfully, "when you could not undertake me. God bless you, dear Friend, wherever you go."

CHAPTER SIX

NIGHTINGALE POWER

Whenever I had anything to do with the authorities at Scutari, I never met with anything but personal courtesy and a wish to reform the evils . . . but through all the departments there was a kind of paralysis, a fear of incurring any responsibility, and a fear of going beyond their instructions.
— Augustus Stafford, MP, *circa* 1855

LORENCE FIRST TRAVELED ACROSS FRANCE, WHERE SHE DID some shopping. Although she had been promised ample supplies in Scutari, she took the precaution of spending some of the *Times* money, and some of her own, on the things she would need most. With winter coming on, she bought portable stoves, and made sure all her nurses had warm shoes. Then the party embarked for the eight-day sea voyage to Turkey.

The ship ran into foul weather and high seas, and Florence was miserably seasick. By the time she reached Constantinople, on November 4, 1854, she could barely stand up. The next morning, clutching their bags and umbrellas, she and her nurses were lowered into small fishing-boats and rowed across the bay to Scutari. With a pack of starving dogs at their heels, they

The Barrack Hospital. Scutari is now a suburb of Istanbul called Üsküdar, and the barracks building holds a military headquarters. The Turkish army and the Turkish Nurses' Association have turned one of its great, square towers into a museum honoring Florence and her nurses.

made their way up a muddy path, past heaps of rubbish and the body of a dead horse, to the Barrack Hospital.

What they found was appalling. The hospital was a vast, filthy building with open sewers running underneath. The courtyard in the center was a mud-wallow piled with garbage. The toilet system was hopelessly blocked up, and germs and the stink of overflowing chamberpots and wooden tubs polluted the medical wards. More than two hundred women – some of them prostitutes, and many of them infected with cholera – were living in the cellars. There were insects, mice, and rats everywhere.

If the rats were finding enough to eat, they were luckier than most of the patients. Bread came in the form of rock-hard biscuits. The army knew that the men would get scurvy if they didn't have vitamin C. Since there was little or no fruit, and there were rarely any vegetables except dried peas, tons of lime juice had been shipped out to prevent the disease. But for months nobody had got around to distributing the juice, and many soldiers had their gums so rotted by scurvy that they couldn't chew the biscuits.

By this time the Barrack Hospital had one kitchen, with thirteen vats for cooking. Animal carcasses were hacked into portions and thrown into boiling water, and then the pieces were handed out to the soldiers. Some got meat; some got bone and gristle. Some got tough, overboiled scraps; some got the last lumps thrown into the pot, still oozing blood. Many of the men were far too sick to gnaw the meat, let alone digest it, but there was almost nothing else: no eggs, no jellies, no custards. These men were starving to death.

As for the famous supplies, where were they? There were still no pillows, and almost no blankets. Most of the men lay on the floor in filthy shirts. Laundry was sent out to be washed by local workers, but often it was only swished in cold water. When the clothes came back, they were still crawling with blood-sucking lice.

Why was the hospital so shamefully mismanaged? In the years since Napoleon's defeat, the government had saved money by cutting back the army's medical department, and the offices of supply and transport. Also, the army bureaucracy was hopelessly tied up in red tape. Every purchase had to be authorized and approved and signed off at several levels, and processed by the office of the Purveyor and the office of the Commissariat, and nothing could be done until the last scrap of paperwork was finished. On one occasion, wounded men were already bedded down in new sheets when a medical inspector, Dr. Cumming, found the paperwork incomplete. He ordered the sheets stripped off and taken away, leaving the men to shiver in the cold. Another time, two shiploads of fresh vegetables were dumped in the sea because the army wasn't quite sure who was supposed to get them.

This photo by Roger Fenton shows supply ships waiting in Balaclava harbor. Because no storehouses had been set up, goods were kept on board until they were needed — and then it was almost impossible to find them. The commander of one steamer complained that "he found the greatest difficulty in getting rid of his cargo, though he well knew how much needed the items were." With so much inefficiency, there was plenty of room for theft and fraud. If something was missing, it might be waiting in a Turkish customs-house, or buried in a ship, or it might have been stolen. Or maybe it had never been bought; maybe someone had simply pocketed the money.

If the physical condition of the hospital was foul, it was no worse than the prevailing mood. The government had ordered the army to allow Florence and her party into the Barrack Hospital, but some of the senior doctors con-

The British had some fine doctors in the Crimea, but the physician in charge, John Hall, was old-fashioned and dictatorial. He disapproved of chloroform, preferring to do operations (even amputations) on wide-awake patients. He had no time for interfering busybodies like researchers, sanitary experts, or — of course — female nurses. He inspected the Scutari hospitals shortly before Florence arrived, and pronounced them in fine order; "nothing is lacking," he said. The junior doctors didn't dare contradict "the fossil," as Florence called him, and he was furious when she disagreed about anything. Dr. Hall was usually at Balaclava, so Florence didn't see him much, but his pride and resentment created endless problems.

sidered the nurses' presence an insult, and a threat to their authority. They lodged all the new arrivals in five small, dirty rooms with no bedding and almost no furniture, plus a kitchen with no table, no food, and no cooking facilities. The women were issued one bowl each, to be used for both washing and drinking, and they were allowed just two cups of water a day; if they used too much for washing, they would have to go without tea.

As for their work, the senior doctors decreed that neither "the Bird" (as they nicknamed Miss Nightingale) nor her nurses would be allowed anywhere near the patients. Let this high-society meddler do nothing at all, let her get bored and go back home where she belonged; that would suit these doctors just fine.

Florence was infuriated by their attitude, but she understood exactly what they were up to. Instead of arguing or making trouble, she set her nurses to housekeeping chores. She assigned some of them to the nearby General Hospital (though they would come back to sleep in the cramped Barrack quarters) and kept the rest with her. The nurses sorted supplies, and improvised shirts, slings, and pillows. They bought foods suited for invalids in Constantinople and cooked them on their portable stoves, even though the doctors wouldn't let the men eat them. And they waited for the tide to turn.

It didn't take long. Ten days before Florence reached Scutari, the British had fought the Battle of Balaclava. This battle included the famous Charge of the Light Brigade, when the vanity and incompetence of the commanders sent a few hundred cavalry charging valiantly against impossible odds. William Russell, the *Times* reporter, described the cannon-fire that cut down the men and their horses: "The whole line of the enemy belched forth, from thirty iron mouths, a flood of smoke and flame, through which hissed the deadly balls." The blunder killed almost three-quarters of the brigade, and is remembered in a famous poem by Tennyson:

Theirs not to reason why,
Theirs but to do and die.
Into the valley of Death
   Rode the six hundred.

Thousands of men wounded at Balaclava were on their way to Scutari by the time Florence got there, and on that same day came the Battle of Inkerman, and another host of casualties. And war wounds were only part of the problem. The weather was frigid, and the rain and snow seemed endless. Between battles, the men besieging Sebastopol lived in leaky tents and stood guard in trenches full of icy slush, with their boots freezing to their feet. Some of them wore knitted hoods that covered their faces, leaving only their eyes showing, so that icicles couldn't grow on their mustaches; today we still call these hoods balaclavas.

A sergeant described the soldiers' misery: "Men would come staggering into the camp from the trenches soaked to the skin and ravenously hungry, when a half-pound of mouldy biscuit would be issued, with the same quantity of salt junk [pork or beef], so hard that one almost wanted a good hatchet to break it. . . . The whole camp was one vast sheet of mud, the trenches in many places knee deep [in mud]; men died at their posts from sheer exhaustion or starvation. . . ."

With the hospital already full, and shiploads of sick and wounded headed for their doorstep, the doctors finally admitted that they needed all the help they could get. They agreed to let the nurses do their job.

Now Florence rolled up her sleeves and really got to work. First things first: she persuaded the orderlies to carry away the stinking chamberpots and empty them. She ordered two hundred scrub brushes and had the floor thoroughly cleaned, and then the nurses sewed up big sacks and stuffed them with straw. As soldiers arrived, they were washed and settled onto these mattresses, and their wounds were tended. For a while her nurses cooked beef broth right by the bedsides, on their portable stoves, and spoon-fed the weakest men – until Dr. Cumming, the same man who had ordered the sheets off the beds, banned all cooking in the wards.

Next came the supply cupboards. Florence ordered trays, clocks, and operating tables. She bought screens so that the men in the wards didn't have to see their comrades under the surgeon's knife. Using the supplies she had brought, and whatever she could get from Constantinople, she began dispensing all kinds of goods: "socks, shirts, knives and forks," she listed, "wooden spoons, tin baths, tables and forms, cabbages and carrots, operating tables, towels and soap. . . ." When twenty-seven thousand shirts were sitting uselessly on a ship, waiting for army paperwork that was weeks away, she handed out fifty thousand from her own stores.

Now, about that food. . . . She turned the small kitchen in the nurses' quarters into an "extra-diet" kitchen where, with the doctors' permission, her nurses could prepare special dishes – "preposterous luxuries," Dr. Hall called

Fleas (like this) and lice lived on the men, and hid in their clothes and bedding. They drank the men's blood, leaving itchy bites and spreading infections. Florence soon dealt with them: she rented a house, had boilers installed, and hired soldiers' wives to stew the clothes and bedding until they were not only clean but pest-free.

them – for men who couldn't eat the hospital fare. Before long, she would have the help of a real chef; Alexis Soyer, a flamboyant young Frenchman, abandoned the banquets he was cooking at a fashionable London club and sailed for Scutari. There he redesigned the entire kitchen system, planning new ovens so that fresh, soft bread could be baked, and invented a teapot that would serve fifty. Soyer transformed the men's miserable rations into food they could actually eat.

"The reign of chaos and old night began to dwindle," noted a Victorian biographer; "order came upon the scene, and common sense, and fore-thought, and decision, radiating out of the little room . . . where, day and night, the Lady Superintendent was at her task." The soldiers adored her. They swallowed their curses, and even their cries of pain, out of respect for her. Many senior officers believed that common soldiers were coarse, immoral brutes who would turn soft if they were decently treated. Florence knew bet-ter; she always cared for the men tenderly, listening to their fears, consoling them. After the war, she would write that tears still came to her eyes when she remembered their "innate dignity, gentleness and chivalry" in the midst of disease and death.

Meanwhile, more help had arrived – more than Florence wanted, that is. Sidney Herbert had promised her that no more nurses would be sent unless she asked for them. Just as she settled in, she was dismayed to learn that someone she knew, Mary Stanley, was about to arrive with a large group. There were fifteen Catholic nuns, nine ladies with no nursing experience, and more than twenty working nurses – some respectable, some disgraceful. But there was no room for these women, and no food or water. Mary Stanley ran out of funds shortly after she got there, and Florence had to feed the group out of her own pocket. Worse yet, their lack of training and discipline might ruin the reputation she was so carefully building up. She wrote a furious letter to Sidney Herbert, threatening to resign, but calmed down after most of the new arrivals were sent to other hospitals. Some were so useless that they were sent home.

As the fight for the fortress of Sebastopol continued, the shiploads of starving, frost-bitten wounded never stopped coming. Many had terrible bedsores – open sores where their skin had rubbed off because they had been lying too long without moving. They suffered dysentery, which caused bloody diarrhea, and typhus, a very dangerous fever transmitted by lice; and, as always, some of them had cholera. Their diseases spread in the wards, and among the medical staff too. In one period of three weeks, four surgeons died. Florence estimated that she was present at two thousand deaths during that first winter.

One small section of the Barrack Hospital lay ruined and empty, and Florence had the idea of rebuilding it to hold more wards. The doctors said her plan would never work; the war would be over long before the paperwork could be done. She appealed to the British ambassador to Turkey, and he seemed to agree to the project, but when the workmen raised their prices he backed out, claiming that he knew nothing about it. Disgusted, Florence paid to rebuild the wing, and fill it with equipment, out of her own money and the *Times* fund. Soon she had beds for another eight hundred men. (Embarrassed by the whole affair, the government eventually paid her back.)

Constantinople was an exotic city of "masses of foliage, of red roofs, divers-hued walls, gables and fretwork, surmounted by a frieze of snow-white minarets with golden summits. . . ." Seduced by luxury and pleasure, some British officials were having much too good a time to bother doing their jobs. One of these was the ambassador, a vain, pompous, ill-tempered man who enjoyed lavish picnics and prided himself on his (very bad) poetry. Although his palatial home was just across the bay from Scutari, he visited the hospitals only once – briefly – during the war.

Early in 1855, the British government was voted out and Sidney Herbert lost his job as war secretary. Lord Panmure, who replaced him, was intelligent and well-meaning but – like Florence's father – too lazy to make decisions that might cause him any trouble. Florence gained a new ally, however; the incoming prime minister was Lord Palmerston, her longtime friend, and Palmerston warned Panmure to show due respect for Miss Nightingale.

With this advice (and some prodding from Florence's other supporters), Panmure sent a sanitary commission – two doctors, a civil engineer, and some

At night, Florence made her rounds of the hospital by lamplight. She had a long walk; although the men lay close together, with just enough space that doctors and nurses could reach them, the rows of beds in the Barrack Hospital stretched four miles (over 6 km). But her famous lamp was not like the one shown here; it was a candle inside an accordion-style paper shade that could be folded flat.

plumbing experts – to examine hospital conditions and fix the worst of the problems. Like Florence, the men of the commission recognized the importance of cleanliness; unlike her, they had the power to carry out the massive improvements she had been demanding. The sewers were finally cleaned. The water supply was improved (among other things, two more dead horses were removed from it). Miles of rat-infested woodwork were torn out. Tons of rotting filth were dug up and carted away.

Within six months of Florence's arrival, the men were being treated, if not well, at least decently. They had a hope of being washed and comforted, of getting their hair combed and their teeth brushed, of having clean clothes and bedding, and food they could keep down. The hospital looked and smelled better, and the new sanitation had slowed down the spread of infections and diseases. The death rate had dropped astonishingly, from 42 percent to just over 2 percent.

❧

Although Florence cared deeply about her patients, and spent long, anguished hours among them, even more of her time was taken up by office work. She answered questions and gave advice, to medical staff, officers, suppliers, and officials of all sorts. She made lists and kept records and wrote reports. Working on nights so cold that the ink froze in her inkwell, she turned out thousands of urgent letters – to friends, politicians, anyone who might help. She dispatched sympathetic notes to the friends and families of the soldiers, often sending home their dying words. She wrote to towns and villages all over Britain, thanking them for their "Free Gifts" – parcels of comforts donated to the soldiers. Charles Bracebridge worried that she was "working herself to death; . . . the attempt to do more will kill her."

She also wrote constantly to Sidney Herbert. She sent him formal reports of progress, to be passed on to the army and government; informal updates for his private information; savage personal notes attacking the filth, the bad food, and almost all the doctors. Herbert passed some of her more polite

William Howard Russell, the reporter whose stories alerted the British people to the horrors of the Crimean War, was the first modern war correspondent — that is, the first journalist assigned specifically to attend a war and tell readers what was really going on. Here, Russell works in his tent (left) while Florence stands in the snow, awaiting more wounded men. Photography was in its early days, and newspapers were illustrated with sketches instead.

accounts to Queen Victoria, who asked that the nurses "tell these poor noble wounded and sick men that *no one* takes a warmer interest or feels *more* for their sufferings or admires their courage and heroism *more* than their Queen." Never one to pass up an opportunity, Florence promptly used the Queen's influence to win her sick soldiers a raise in pay.

✦

How did Florence achieve so much? Not through noise and fury, but "by strict method, by stern discipline, by rigid attention to detail, by ceaseless labour, by the fixed determination of an indomitable will." She spoke calmly and quietly, and those who worked with her said she never raised her voice, but she put so much resolve and authority into her words that somehow – sooner or later – she almost always got her way. "Nightingale power," the men called it. "If she were at our head, we should be in Sebastopol next week," they said. Once, when a doctor assured her that something could not be done, her answer was simple: "But it must be done." And it was.

CHAPTER SEVEN

THE LADY WITH THE LAMP

Such a head! I wish we had her at the War Office!
— Queen Victoria, 1856

ITH THE SCUTARI HOSPITALS CLEANED UP AND RUNNING more efficiently, Florence set out to inspect the hospitals in the Crimea. Her ship reached Balaclava in May 1855. By this time she was famous among the soldiers, and she thrilled the troops besieging Sebastopol by visiting the battle-lines and posing gracefully on a gun battery, indifferent as always to danger. Then she toured the General Hospital, to see what needed work.

What didn't need work? The hospital was disgraceful, with dirty premises, sloppy practices, and careless nurses. But her attempts to improve it met with defiance, for this was the territory of her worst enemies, including the arrogant Dr. Hall, and Mary Stanley's nurses. They seized on the fact that Florence had been named superintendent for all the British army hospitals *in Turkey*; the Crimea was just outside Turkey, and therefore, they said, none of her business.

They had good reason to resist her: their procedures were scandalously unprofessional. Some of the "lady nurses" were living in luxury, cooking cozy dinners for their favorite officers and helping themselves to the Free Gifts sent for the wounded. With Dr. Hall setting the example, the medical staff treated Florence with contempt and obstructed her at every step. As she prepared to maneuver around them, she was struck down – not by her enemies but by a terrible sickness that the doctors called Crimean fever (it was probably typhus).

If Florence had stayed in the filth and pollution of the General Hospital, she would almost certainly have died. But she was sent instead to Castle Hospital – a collection of huts, supervised by an experienced nurse, on the

CHURCH AGAINST CHURCH

In the 1850s there was bitter rivalry between the various churches in Britain. Florence – who had been raised as an Anglican – managed to control her own nurses despite their religious differences, and one of the Catholic nuns, Mother Bermondsey, became a dear friend. But Mary Stanley's party had brought jealousy and rebellion. Mary Stanley was in the process of becoming Catholic and had all the zeal of the newly converted. Mother Bridgeman, the leader of the Catholic nuns in Mary Stanley's group, was a defiant religious crusader who would take no orders from Florence. (Florence called her Mother Brickbat.) The result was endless bickering and backstabbing, and ridiculous accusations against Florence. Dr. Hall sided with Mother Bridgeman, and used the nurses' rivalry in his own war against Florence, while newspapers at home wrote up the most trivial incidents as shocking scandals. Meanwhile, Mary Stanley avoided the hospital – it was such an unpleasant place – and paid social calls in Constantinople instead. In February 1855, she made a brief and disastrous attempt to run a small hospital on her own. In March – just three months after arriving – she sailed for home, leaving Florence to deal with the problems she had created.

heights above Balaclava harbor. For weeks she suffered a dangerous fever and hallucinations. Even in the madness of her delirium, she couldn't rest; she scribbled wildly, solving imaginary problems, churning out notes and orders in spidery handwriting. Her lovely hair was chopped short. Doctors feared for her life. When word of her illness spread, soldiers on the front lines grieved for her, while patients at Scutari turned their faces to the wall and wept. But at last the fever and delirium passed, and she began to recover.

Frail and feeble – badly underweight, unable to feed herself, barely able to talk – Florence defied the doctors, who said she should go home to England, and insisted on staying in the Crimea. "If I go, all this will go to pieces," she wrote to Parthe. As a compromise, she returned to Scutari but spent a few weeks recovering in a private home. By August she was back at work in the Barrack Hospital.

By now the nursing was the least of her problems. With the hospital running well, some of the doctors resented her and felt she was no longer needed. The nurses were a constant source of trouble: some died, some got drunk, some got married. One very plump nurse was invited to join a Turkish dignitary's harem; Florence had to explain that her nurses were not for sale. The

One night, as Florence lay in her sickbed, a cloaked figure rode up to her door and said that he was "only a soldier" but he must see her. It was Lord Raglan, commander-in-chief of the British forces. Raglan was a brave and experienced soldier. When his arm had been amputated (without anesthetic) after the Battle of Waterloo, he had ordered the men to bring back his severed limb: "There is a ring my wife gave me on the finger." He tried hard to do his duty, but he was almost seventy and the job was too much for him. Just a month after visiting Florence, he died.

woman in charge of the Free Gifts stole them shamelessly; when she was sent home quietly, in an effort to avoid scandal, she announced to the world that it was Florence who was misusing the gifts. Mary Stanley sided with Florence's accuser. There was a formal investigation, and Florence wasted many hours defending herself against this petty revenge.

There was also a whole new set of problems with the soldiers. Now that their physical needs were more or less met, they were recovering in an atmosphere of boredom and depression. Many of them couldn't read or write, so the days passed very slowly. They resented the officers, who had comfortable quarters and good food, and servants to care for them.

Although the army offered to send part of the soldiers' pay home to their families, the men (not surprisingly) didn't trust the system, and believed they would be cheated. Many spent their wages on drinking and gambling instead. After all, there wasn't much else to do.

Knowing that the men were deeply worried about their loved ones, Florence started her own money-order system. She accepted whatever money the men gave her, and sent it home to her uncle Sam Smith, who mailed payments to the men's families. The families were reassured and better off, and the men were relieved of both their worries and their drinking money. The scheme was so successful that the government finally took it over, setting up an official remittance system that the men could trust.

Before going to Balaclava, Florence had furnished a room at Scutari where the men could read or play games to forget their troubles. She had even tried to hire a teacher for the men who couldn't read, but army authorities had rejected the idea. "You are spoiling the brutes," said the commanding officer. Now a more sympathetic officer was in charge, and Scutari soon had a new coffee shop and recreation center, and four schools with professional teachers. People at home donated books, maps, writing materials, and amusements, and Florence's family helped organize them into shipments: "chess, footballs, other

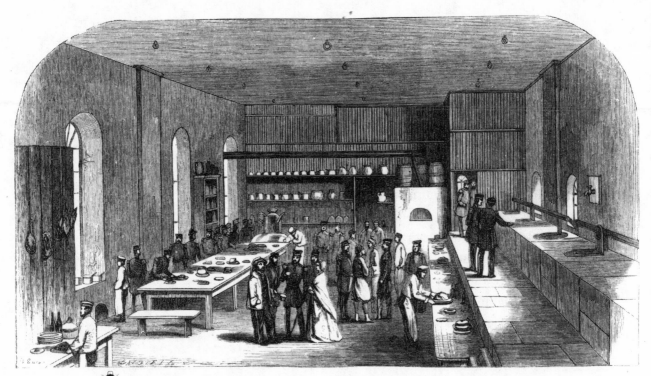

*The new kitchens at Scutari. Alexis Soyer was a cook after Florence's own heart —
dedicated not to gourmet flourishes, but to cooking "in the most nutritive and economical
manner for great quantities of people," she said. Soyer's teapot for fifty is at the back of the
table on the left.*

games," listed Parthe, ". . . a stereoscope (very fine!), plays for acting, music. . . ."
Florence wrote happily that the soldiers were attending lectures; starting
singing groups; staging plays; and competing at football, dominoes, and chess.

Unfortunately, her successes at Scutari were overshadowed by the problems
at Balaclava. Kitchens planned by Alexis Soyer had still not been built there.
When Florence hired a cook for Balaclava, at her own expense, he was sent
away. When she tried to replace a fussy, weak-willed woman running the
General Hospital, Dr. Hall appointed the woman to run a newer hospital

instead. Meanwhile, Mother Bridgeman used her nursing sisters wherever and however she pleased, with Dr. Hall's support, and one of Hall's colleagues announced to the War Office that Florence's nurses were "dishonest, extravagant, disobedient, inefficient, and immoral."

The Bracebridges had sailed for home in the summer of 1855, worn out by all the hardships and stresses, and Aunt Mai came to take their place. She burst into tears when she saw how pale and weak her niece had become, but she couldn't persuade Florence to take care of herself. "I never saw a greater picture of exhaustion than Flo last night at ten," she reported. "'Oh, do go to bed,' I said. 'How can I; I have all these letters to write,' pointing to the divan covered with papers. 'Write them tomorrow.' 'Tomorrow will bring its own work.' And she sat up the greater part of the night."

In October 1855, Florence returned to the Crimean peninsula. By this time the Russians had abandoned the fortress of Sebastopol, and the end of the war was in sight. But the hospitals were still overloaded with patients, and she was determined to win the cooperation of Dr. Hall and Mother Bridgeman. Just as she thought she was making progress, her efforts were sabotaged.

Now that he was back in England, Charles Bracebridge was trying to defend Florence by blaming Dr. Hall and his allies for everything wrong in the Crimean hospitals. News of his accusations soon reached Dr. Hall. He was outraged and blamed Florence for the attack, but she was almost as angry as he was. "Christ was betrayed by one, but my cause has been betrayed by everyone – ruined, destroyed . . . ," she wrote, adding that Dr. Hall "is dead against me. . . . He descends to every meanness to make my position more difficult." The government did nothing to support her. She was still weak from her illness, and suffering headaches, earaches, eye problems, rheumatism, and laryngitis. At the end of November, when she rushed back to Scutari to handle an outbreak of cholera, she felt utterly defeated.

Florence in the wards of Scutari. Despite her ailments, she was always back at work as soon as possible. Mrs. Gaskell described her as "so excessively gentle in voice, manner, and movement, that one never feels the unbendableness of her character when one is near her. Her powers are astonishing."

By now, though, "The Lady with the Lamp" was virtually a saint in the eyes of the British people. Popular songs trumpeted her virtues; one declared: "May God give her strength, and her heart never fail, / One of Heaven's best gifts is Miss Nightingale." Her life story was printed and sold for a penny a copy. She appeared in souvenir china figurines, and as a mannequin at Madame Tussaud's wax museum. Her name was given to a street, a lifeboat, and a racehorse. The letters of her name were jumbled into an anagram: *Flit on, cheering angel.* Across the country, baby girls were being named Florence, in her honor. She was often compared to Joan of Arc. (She found wry amusement in that comparison: "There is not an official who would not burn me like Joan of Arc if he could. . . .")

With so much adoration in the air, some of Florence's friends – including Sidney Herbert and Richard Monckton Milnes – formed a committee and started a Nightingale Fund. The idea was that people could thank Florence for her work by sending donations. Once the war was over, Florence could use the money to set up her own nursing school.

The Sultan of Turkey showed his appreciation by sending Florence a diamond bracelet, as well as some money for her nurses. The Queen wanted to honor Florence too, so Prince Albert designed a diamond brooch with the cross of Saint George (patron saint of England) set out in red enamel, and the motto "Blessed are the merciful." Florence wrote to thank the royal couple for the gift and – lecturing as usual – included a brief analysis of the causes of drunkenness among soldiers.

In the spring of 1856, Florence was once again distraught. After sending the Sanitary Commission to Scutari, Lord Panmure had sent a Commissariat Commission to Balaclava. The two members – Colonel Tulloch from the Royal Engineers, and a doctor named Sir John McNeill – had investigated the shortages and supply problems. They had improved the kitchens, documented the stupidity and inefficiency that had caused so many deaths, and named those who were most to blame. But the men they accused were very senior officers, and most of them had already been promoted and rewarded for their "services." Rather than cause embarrassment, Panmure let the army sweep the McNeill–Tulloch report under the carpet. Two of the guilty parties, including Dr. Hall, were appointed Knight Commanders of the Order of the Bath (KCB). "Knights of the Crimean Burial grounds," seethed Florence;

"Can we hear of the promotion of the men who caused this colossal calamity, we who saw it?"

❧❧

Worn out by the endless lies and conspiracies of her enemies, Florence again pleaded with the War Department to uphold her authority, and to assist her in her "ever recurring and exhausting struggle for every inch of the ground secured to me by the original agreement." But now she got support from a surprising quarter. Exasperated by all the arguments and scandals over the nurses, Lord Panmure had sent a special envoy – in effect, a spy – to find out what was really going on. The envoy's report was uncompromising: Florence was absolutely right, he announced, and she must have the confirmation she was asking for. In March 1856 the War Department finally issued a crisp state-ment noting that *apparently* the medical officers did "not correctly comprehend Miss Nightingale's position," and pointedly reminding them that Florence was in charge of *all* the army's female nurses.

A romanticized painting by Henrietta Rae shows Florence looking as if she has stepped out of the Bible. The poet Henry Wadsworth Longfellow captured the adoration she inspired among the soldiers in a poem written in 1857. The poem is called "Santa Filomena" – Italian for "Saint Nightingale."

> *Lo! in that house of misery*
> *A lady with a lamp I see*
> *   Pass through the glimmering gloom,*
> *   And flit from room to room.*
>
> *And slow, as in a dream of bliss,*
> *The speechless sufferer turns to kiss*
> *   Her shadow, as it falls*
> *   Upon the darkening walls.*

By the time this declaration reached the war zone, Florence had gone back to Balaclava, taking some nurses for a small new hospital. She was still hoping to settle her differences with Mother Bridgeman, but the mother superior rejected her proposals and resigned, sailing for England and taking her nuns with her. Florence was left to oversee all the hospitals in the area. They were miles apart, and there were almost no roads, but she managed to visit them anyway. On a horse or in a carriage – on foot, if need be – she crossed the countryside, often arriving well after dark. "I have seen that lady stand for hours at the top of a bleak rocky mountain near the hospitals," marveled Alexis Soyer, "giving her instructions while the snow was falling heavily."

The General Hospital was still filthy and badly run, much as Scutari had been on her arrival, and the patients were covered with bedsores and lice. Florence and her nurses began the weary process of scrubbing the building and washing the men. Bitter in defeat, Dr. Hall – now Sir John Hall – kept up his old tricks. He left Florence locked out in the snow for hours. He squabbled over everything, blocked her requests for supplies, and even tried to starve her out. (Small chance of that; Florence had anticipated his meanness, and had brought along stoves and enough food for her nurses.) There is a story that when a large rat appeared over a patient's bed one day, she smashed it dead with her umbrella. She must have wished she could dispose of all her enemies that easily.

The victory over Dr. Hall was gratifying, but it was too little, too late. By the end of April, the Crimean War was over. At the end of June, Florence returned to Scutari to close down the nursing operation there. She said fond farewells to the good nurses, doing what she could to help them: arranging holidays, finding them jobs, even slipping them a little money.

As the last patients headed home, she thought bitterly of all those who would stay for ever: "I am a bad mother to come home and leave you in your Crimean graves – 73 per cent in 8 regiments in 6 months from disease alone – who thinks of that now?" A quarter of a million men had died on the allied side alone – about a third of them in battle, and the rest from infection and disease. Far, far more would have died without the extraordinary labors and determination of Florence Nightingale.

But she had done more than save lives. She had shown that soldiers were decent men who responded to kindness and fairness, and deserved respect for their bravery, loyalty, and stoicism. She had demonstrated that cleanliness and nutrition were essential to the healing process. And she had proved, for once and for all, that nursing was a noble and vitally important profession – and that women did a wonderful job of it.

Britain was planning a lavish welcome. The government offered a warship to sail her home. Regiments competed to have their marching bands hail her arrival. There were plans for speeches, parades, triumphal arches. The Queen wrote Florence a private letter reminding her "how warm my admiration is for your services, which are fully equal to those of my dear and brave soldiers. . . ." But Florence and Aunt Mai traveled secretly, calling themselves Mrs. and Miss Smith. When they reached Paris, Aunt Mai stayed on and Florence headed for England on her own.

On August 7, 1856, Britain's heroine stepped off the train alone at a little country railroad station and walked across the fields to Lea Hurst to see her family. At the age of thirty-six, she was weary and heartsick. She was little more than skin and bone, and so ill she could barely look at food. For all the lives she had saved, she had very nearly lost her own.

CHAPTER EIGHT

THE LABOR AND THE WOUNDS

*I stand at the altar of the murdered men and while I live
I shall fight their cause.*

— Florence Nightingale

S SOON AS WORD GOT OUT THAT FLORENCE WAS HOME, SHE was awash in gifts and requests. Would she accept an award here, make a speech there, attend a meeting someplace else? The answer was no. She was haunted by the horrors she had seen. She was frail and exhausted, and the sight of food still made her ill. Her doctors feared for her life and warned her to do nothing but rest. "I cannot believe that she will live long," wrote Parthe.

After the first family welcome, Florence had moved into a suite at the Burlington Hotel in London. Fanny and Parthe were there with her – reveling in her fame and glory, being utterly useless, yet insisting that they were there only to help poor Flo.

For her part, Florence wished they would go home. After all, she had work to do. There was more than £40,000 in the Nightingale Fund – several million

The worn-out crusader after her illnesses during the war. When her father came to see her, he was horrified. "Her days may be numbered," he told her mother. Though her dress and cap seem fancy by modern standards, they were severe compared to the fashions of the day.

dollars, in today's values – which she could use to set up a school of nursing, but she had other things on her mind. Of the thousands of men dead in the Crimean War, most had been killed by carelessness and stupidity. For every man who died of his wounds, another seven had died from disease. And British soldiers were still fighting and dying in other corners of the world. The entire army medical system had to be changed – and if she didn't change it, who would?

There was one invitation she could not refuse. Queen Victoria and Prince Albert were on holiday at Balmoral Castle, in Scotland, and they asked her to come and explain her theories to them. Florence stayed with a friend who lived near Balmoral, and had several visits with the royal couple. They were impressed by her arguments, and by the breadth of her knowledge. They wanted to help. But while they had a great deal of influence, they had no direct power to change the army medical system.

But the man who did have that power – the war secretary, Lord Panmure – was coming to visit Balmoral. The Queen asked Florence to come back during his stay. Both Florence and Sidney Herbert felt that the meeting would achieve nothing; although Panmure was an honorable man, he had the habit of ignoring problems and hoping they would go away. But the Queen insisted, and Florence obeyed – and "Nightingale power" worked its magic once again. Florence and Lord Panmure found common ground on three subjects.

The first was the Royal Victoria Military Hospital, which was to be built at Netley, overlooking the river near Southampton. Panmure said he would send Florence the plans, in case she could suggest ways to improve the design.

The second was Florence's idea of a new army medical school. Most army doctors were surgeons, trained to treat cuts and broken bones and other problems they could see and feel. Many still ridiculed the claim that unwashed hands and soiled equipment could make a grown man sick. Florence wanted future army doctors to know all the latest ideas about sanitation. Panmure admitted that this was a good idea.

The third and most important issue was more difficult. Florence was determined that there should be a Royal Commission – a full government investigation – to report on the hospital disasters of the Crimean War. She wanted the members appointed to the Royal Commission to pinpoint the problems, and pave the way for a top-to-bottom remodeling of the army medical system. Such an investigation would be furiously resisted by the guilty parties and their supporters, and it would embarrass people in high places. All the same, Panmure seemed to accept the idea. He asked Florence to send him a detailed explanation of everything that was wrong, and how it should be fixed.

Frail as she was, she again turned into a whirlwind. She worked her way through the masses of reports she had compiled at Scutari, with her proposals for reorganizing the supplies, the cooking, the staff, the record-keeping, the medical training – in short, the entire system. She sent letters to other experts, asking for their opinions. She compared statistics and wrote up her conclusions. She visited powerful friends, urging them to join her cause.

While Florence worked night and day, her mother and sister still insisted on "helping" her at the Burlington. She wrote acidly to Clarkey about how certain people could "lie on the sofa all day, doing absolutely nothing, and persuade themselves and others that they are the victims of their self-devotion for another who is dying of overwork."

Lord Panmure sent Florence the plans for the hospital at Netley, as promised. She found the design hopelessly outdated and impractical. She sent back a point-by-point critique, suggesting an open design for plenty of fresh air, and quoting examples and statistics from hospitals across Europe. But it turned out that the hospital was already being built. The drastic changes she demanded would be expensive and embarrassing. Her advice had come too late.

It's no wonder Fanny and Parthe were so useless; look at the fashions in Godey's Lady's Book, *a women's magazine of the time. By the 1850s, crinolines of stiff horsehair (crin is French for "horsehair") were all the rage. When early crinolines proved too bulky, ladies adopted the cage crinoline, a hollow frame like a giant birdcage. "It was difficult to fit through doorways . . . , embarrassing on windy days if the wind caught it underneath, and you could fall down steps in it if you weren't careful," noted one author. Florence refused to wear such a ridiculous contraption. "Compelled by her dress," she sniffed, "every woman now either shuffles or waddles — only a man can cross the floor of a sick room without shaking it!"*

She visited the Prime Minister and told him the whole story, and he tried to halt the construction, but Panmure held firm. Although some of Florence's smaller suggestions were adopted, the hospital was a grandiose bungle. Still, the episode reminded Panmure that Florence was well connected, relentlessly stubborn, and — worst of all — usually right.

❦

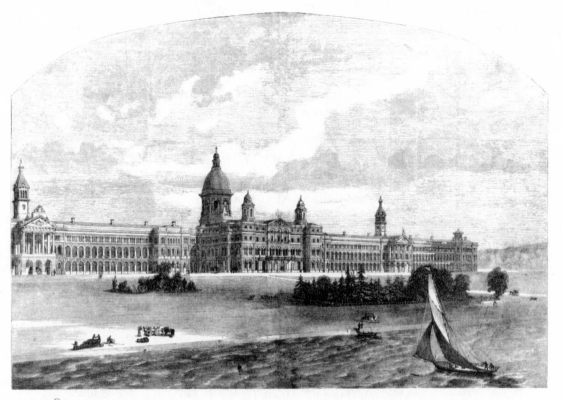

The elegant but badly designed Royal Victoria Military Hospital. Lord Palmerston agreed with Florence that the patients' needs had been "sacrificed to the vanity of the architect," and said he would as soon toss the building into the river as have it finished the way it was planned, but it was built anyway.

As for the Royal Commission, Florence knew Panmure would rather avoid the scandal of an investigation – or, failing that, would brush aside its findings. The commission would not succeed unless the people appointed to it were prominent, resolute, and tireless. Though she would gladly have carried the entire project on her own shoulders, army bureaucrats would automatically reject anything she suggested. In any case, at a time when women weren't even allowed to vote, it was out of the question for a woman to hold such a post. Florence would have to hitch her cause to a team of carefully chosen "horses," and ride behind them, plying her whip.

As her lead "horse" – the committee's chairman – she chose Sidney Herbert. He was weary and unwell, but Florence demanded his services and he agreed to do the job. Another leading member was John Sutherland, a public health expert and one of the doctors on the Sanitary Commission sent to Scutari; he was now Florence's personal physician.

Pressured by all the people who were afraid of the Royal Commission, Panmure stalled in his usual fashion. Months went by and nothing happened. Florence was sickened by his shilly-shallying. Her opponents, she said, "have all fed their children on the fat of the land and dressed them in velvet and silk. . . . I have had to see my children dressed in a dirty blanket and an old pair of regimental trousers, and to see them fed on raw salt meat, and nine thousand of my children are lying . . . in their forgotten graves." In February, 1857, desperate to get the commission going before people lost interest in the Crimean War, Florence threatened to enlist her most powerful ally: the British people.

"Three months from this day I publish my experience of the Crimean campaign," she declared to Sidney Herbert. If she carried out this alarming threat – naming names and listing blunders with her usual thoroughness – it would be a disaster for the government. The only way to keep her quiet was to give her what she wanted. In May the Royal Commission on the Sanitary Condition of the Army was finally at work, and Florence said no more about publishing her experiences.

Needless to say, much of the evidence for the commission would come from Florence herself. During the long, cold nights at Scutari, she had been working on a massive analysis of the army medical system. Now she completed this work, calling it *Notes on Matters Affecting the Health, Efficiency and Hospital Administration of the British Army*. It was an extraordinary feat of work, almost a thousand pages long, and bolstered with tables and flurries of statistics.

Florence refused to testify in person before the commission; her fame and popularity would only enrage her opponents. Instead she received written questions, and extracted thirty pages' worth of answers from her manuscript. She interviewed other witnesses, helping them with their testimony and advising Sidney Herbert on what to ask them. Dr. Sutherland marveled at her "strength and clearness of mind, her extraordinary powers joined with her benevolence of spirit. She is one of the most gifted creatures God ever made."

Despite her anger, she refrained from blaming even the worst offenders, insisting that "the system which placed them where they were is the point to be considered." Her message was simple: good soldiers were being killed by the army as surely as if they were being lined up and shot. Instead of being treated after they got sick, they should be kept healthy. If the army wanted to win its wars, it would have to allow the "brutes" in the front lines decent clothes, food, living quarters, and sanitation. "Our soldiers enlist to death in the barracks," she declared, and this accusation was trumpeted by the newspapers.

For three months, Florence, Sidney Herbert, and John Sutherland worked on their report. Fearing that her life was running out, she drove both men without mercy. She dismissed Herbert's spells of sickness and depression as "fancies." Whenever Dr. Sutherland tried to skip a meeting, pleading ill health

One of the inquiries into the disasters of the Crimean War. Despite all the talk and ceremony, most of the people involved were still hoping to hush up the scandal.

or foul weather, she harried him until he agreed to come. Once, when he put his foot down and refused, she collapsed into a faint; the poor man not only came, but apologized profusely.

The commission's report was finished in September 1857. To save face, Lord Panmure was already acting on some of its recommendations. He had set up four committees to study four main reforms: improving the army buildings; keeping statistics so that problems would be more obvious; reforming the army medical department; and starting up the army medical school that Florence wanted. Sidney Herbert would be the chairman of all four committees.

By this time, though, Florence's poor health had caught up with her. She was troubled by a pounding heart. She had trouble breathing and sleeping, and was living mostly on tea because she couldn't face solid food. Obsessed with work, and infuriated by Fanny and Parthe – who imagined themselves exhausted from "putting flowers into water," said Florence – she collapsed on August 11. She retreated to the health spa at Malvern, taking just one servant with her; "I must be alone, quite alone," she said.

The doctor at Malvern was alarmed by how quickly her heart was beating, and warned her to stay in bed until her heartbeat was back to normal. Dr. Sutherland also begged her to stay at Malvern and rest. "You must have new blood or you can't work," he pointed out, "and new blood can't be made out of tea." Instead of being grateful for his concern, she sent back a furious letter comparing herself to a little dead owl being pecked to pieces. Poor Dr. Sutherland; he was the one being pecked to bits.

Once again Aunt Mai was called in, and by September Florence was well enough to be back at work at the Burlington. But Aunt Mai went with her, and when Parthe tried to move in, she was told to stay somewhere else. Florence had so much to do, and believed she had so little time left to do it.

While Florence was keeping her two colleagues from their homes and their wives, another man found himself turned away. Sir Harry Verney was courting her. Like Richard Monckton Milnes, Verney seemed an eminently suitable match. He was fifty-six years old, a widower with four children, a Member of Parliament. He was intelligent, idealistic, charming, and so noble-looking that people stopped to stare at him in the street. He was admirably reform-minded, and used his considerable wealth to build cottages and schools for poor country laborers.

Sir Harry finally proposed to Florence, but her views of marriage had not changed. She turned him down, and Fanny invited the disappointed suitor to Embley – perhaps to console him, or perhaps to make sure *this* potential

BIRTH AND DEATH BEFORE MODERN MEDICINE

The first few years of childhood used to be a perilous time. Consider the children of Mary, Lady Verney – one of Sir Harry Verney's relatives. She was married when she was thirteen, in 1629.

1632	A daughter is born, and dies.
1633	Another daughter is born, and dies.
1634	A daughter, Anna Maria, is born.
1636	A son, Edmund, is born.
1638	A daughter, Peggy, is born. Anna Maria dies.
1640	A son, Jack, is born.
1647	A son is born, and dies. Peggy dies.

In 1650, Mary died of tuberculosis. She was thirty-four. Of her seven children, only Jack and Edmund outlived her – and Jack was crippled by rickets, owing to a lack of vitamin D.

son-in-law didn't get away. In any case, in June 1858 Parthenope Nightingale would become Lady Harry Verney, and over the years Sir Harry would become a trusted friend and advisor to the sister-in-law he had first hoped to marry.

Aunt Mai remained at the Burlington, neglecting her own home and family to care for Florence during what everyone assumed to be her final days. Arthur Clough, a well-known young scholar and poet who was married to Mai's daughter Blanche, came every day to run errands for the women. "I hope you will not regret the manner of my death," Florence wrote to Herbert in November, and she drew up her will. In December she made arrangements for her burial.

Army reform was moving at a snail's pace. Senior officers and civil servants fought fiercely to defend their territory, firing off paperwork as ammunition. Florence returned their fire. She wrote a pamphlet titled *Mortality in the British Army*. She sent copies of her thousand-page manuscript, accompanied by personal letters, to everyone of influence, from the Queen down. She bullied a host of experts into writing magazine articles about reform, and then bullied magazine editors into printing the articles.

In February 1858, Lord Palmerston's government was voted out of office, and all seemed lost. Fifteen months later, though, Palmerston was voted in again, and he moved Panmure out of the War Office and put Sidney Herbert back in charge. Herbert worked feverishly to make up for lost time – visiting barracks across the country, ordering improvements, planning reading-rooms for the soldiers, starting a cooking school for army chefs.

Herbert was also determined to get the long-promised army medical school begun. Orders were issued: classrooms must be furnished, laboratories set up, equipment installed. In September 1860, the first ten students arrived

Gradually, the improvements demanded by Florence came into effect. By 1868 the soldiers at Aldershot Camp, in England, were enjoying this handsome reading-room. New rules decreed that army camps should have libraries, coffee shops, classrooms, and sports facilities. The men who fought Britain's wars were finally being treated like human beings, rather than mindless brutes.

at the school and found – empty rooms. The orders were lost in the usual swamp of paperwork, and nothing had been done. By October, though, the school was up and running.

HOW TO BUILD A HOSPITAL

Notes on Hospitals shows the breadth of Florence's expertise; she had an opinion on everything.

Location: "Self-draining, gravelly, or sandy subsoils are best. River banks, estuary shores, valleys, marshy or muddy ground, ought to be avoided."

Design: "Generally the distance between the pavilions should be greater than twice their height in low confined localities, where there is not a free external movement of the air."

Water supply: "Hard water, containing sulphates or carbonates, is unfit for most hospital purposes – especially so for dressing wounds. Filtered rain water is generally the best. . . ."

Lighting: "Operating theatres are best lighted by a good large skylight and a steady northern light from one large window, quite up to the ceiling. . . ."

Construction materials: "The objection to [plaster] is its being porous, and its faculty of absorbing emanations from the sick. . . . When ward walls and ceilings become fouled in this way, hospital diseases are very apt to invade the wards."

Bathrooms: "A lavatory table with a row of sunk white porcelain basins, with outlet tubes and plugs, each basin supplied with hot and cold water, should be placed in the same compartment. . . ."

Furniture: "All bedsteads for hospital use should be of wrought iron, frequently painted of a light cheerful colour. . . . A head shelf to the bed is useful."

Menu: "Usually this consists of soups, farinaceous preparations, including puddings, stewed vegetables, roast joints, baked meat . . . (there should be no frying in a hospital, except for fish. . . .)"

Meanwhile, Florence was also working to improve public hospitals. In 1859 she published a book based on the many hospitals she had toured, and on her correspondence with hundreds of builders and suppliers. She described the filth and overcrowding of public hospitals, and the bad food and unskilled nurses, and all the other problems. She pointed out the obvious: the first duty of a hospital was "that it should do the sick no harm." The book established her as an international expert on hospitals, and she was asked to review building plans from around the world. She was consulted by the King of Portugal, the Queen of Holland, and the government of India.

With her passion for statistics, she found it exasperating that hospitals made up their own ways of classifying diseases. How could they compare treatments and results if they couldn't agree on what they were treating? How could they figure out what worked and what didn't? With the help of Dr. William Farr, an expert on medical statistics, she designed statistical sheets and sent them to hospitals across the country. Many of the hospitals agreed to collect information according to her system, and to publish their statistics once a year.

By this time, she had come back to the idea of opening a nursing school. She couldn't run the school herself – she wasn't well enough, and anyway she had too much else to do – but she could set it up, and keep an eye on the people who did run it. With this subject on her mind, she published *Notes on Nursing*, an informal, no-nonsense guide to cleanliness and health in the home, and the care of children and invalids. The book was translated into French, Italian, and German, and sold millions of copies around the world.

Not long after, she also finished a long manuscript of religious philosophy called *Suggestions for Thought*, and sent copies to her intellectual friends. Florence had never found a church she was happy with. She was especially bothered by the idea that religion meant seeking your own salvation; was that any more noble, she wondered, than seeking your own dinner? As well, she knew that many working-class people had drifted away from the traditional churches, and were living without any religion at all. In her manuscript she proposed a

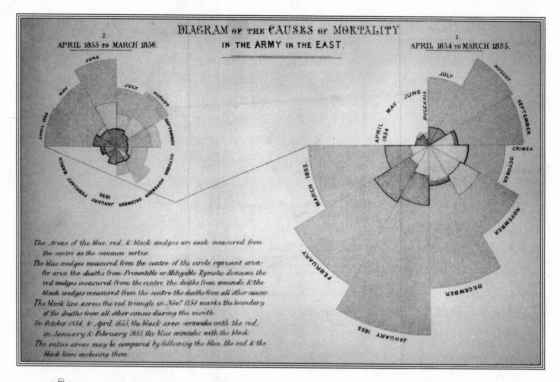

DIAGRAM of the CAUSES of MORTALITY
IN THE ARMY IN THE EAST.

2.
APRIL 1855 to MARCH 1856.

1.
APRIL 1854 to MARCH 1855.

The Areas of the blue, red, & black wedges are each measured from
the centre as the common vertex.

The blue wedges measured from the centre of the circle represent area
for area the deaths from Preventible or Mitigable Zymotic diseases, the
red wedges measured from the centre the deaths from wounds, & the
black wedges measured from the centre the deaths from all other causes.

The black line across the red triangle in Nov.r 1854 marks the boundary
of the deaths from all other causes during the month.

In October 1854, & April 1855, the black area coincides with the red,
in January & February 1855, the blue coincides with the black.

The entire areas may be compared by following the blue, the red & the
black lines enclosing them.

Florence knew that not everyone enjoyed statistics as much as she did, so she illustrated her writings with ingenious colored charts – a technique almost unknown at the time. This three-color chart compares deaths from various causes during the Crimean War, month by month. The very wide outer ring shows how many men died from disease. In 1858 Florence became the first female member of the Statistical Society of London.

new religion, based on spiritual love and mankind's natural harmony with God. Her friends had mixed reactions. Most praised her ideas, but some found her arguments disorganized, or at least poorly expressed.

Arthur Clough sent a copy to Benjamin Jowett, an Anglican clergyman and a brilliant professor of Greek at Oxford University. Although Jowett had misgivings about the writing, he became a lifelong friend of Florence's, and it is said that he even asked her to marry him. As for the book, it was privately printed – it took up three volumes – and set aside.

❦

While Florence agonized over the health of people in general, she could be heartless to those around her. She herself worked tirelessly despite being so weak. Why should she disrupt her efforts for other people's problems? For some time Sam Smith had been trying to get Aunt Mai and Arthur Clough home again; he had been deprived of his wife for two years, and Blanche was worried about her husband's health. Florence collapsed once again, and insisted that she couldn't do without them. In the spring of 1860, Aunt Mai – who had been attending Florence's "deathbed" for more than two years – insisted on going home. Florence took this as a betrayal, and was so angry that she broke off her friendship with her faithful aunt.

Florence's cousin Hilary Bonham Carter took Mai's place for a while. Hilary was a year younger than Florence, and in the years when Florence's ambitions were being resisted by her mother, Hilary had also been frustrated. She was a talented artist who longed for professional training, but her family insisted she stay home and behave like a proper young lady. Now Florence realized that she herself was an obstacle in her cousin's path. Hilary was too good an artist to waste her life on "letter writing and house-keeping," said Florence, and she sent her away.

A month later, Florence lost her remaining assistant. Arthur Clough became very ill. He went to Italy to recover, and died there.

In December 1860, Sidney Herbert's health became much worse, and he broke the bad news to Florence: he was dying of kidney disease. The doctors said that if he stopped work at once, and retired to his beloved family and his beautiful estate, he might live for some time; if he kept working, the pressure would kill him. Yet he knew as well as Florence that the commission's work would not succeed without him. What was he to do?

Torn between her feelings for her old friend, and her need for his work, Florence found a convenient answer: she rejected the doctors' opinions. "I don't believe there is anything in your constitution which makes it evident that disease is getting the upper hand," she announced. With that settled, she and Liz persuaded Herbert to drop his other responsibilities but to remain at the War Office. He worked frantically to complete the reforms, but he was plagued by illness; Liz took him from specialist to specialist, hoping for a miracle. Meanwhile, Florence still denied his illness – "Almost all London physicians are quacks," she said – and pushed him without mercy.

In June 1861, Herbert said he could go on no longer. She blustered that he could work for many years yet, and accused him of being a quitter. Within weeks he was dead, at the age of fifty-one.

Florence was shattered by his death. Their relationship had been a strange one, close and intense yet with no suggestion of romance. In all the years they had worked together, united by their sense of purpose, they had never stopped squabbling. She had nagged him, blamed him, complained about him. He had called her impatient, short-tempered, and full of exaggerations. They had struggled against impossible odds, driving themselves as hard as they drove each other.

Now their fears were realized: one by one, most of the reforms they had worked for were overturned by their enemies. Although Florence fought a rearguard action through her remaining allies, none of them had the strength and influence of her lost champion. "The dogs have trampled on his dead body," she grieved. "We have lost the battle. Now all is over."

But although they had been unable to carry out their great plans, many improvements had been made. More important, they had introduced a new tide of thought, inside and outside the War Office. A number of their disciples were in positions of power, and would continue their work. The changes they had fought for – respect for the common soldier, and decent living conditions, and good medical care – would come in time. They would just take a little longer. Perhaps Florence found comfort in Arthur Clough's poem comparing the slow progress of victory to the unstoppable tide of the "main" (sea). "Say not the struggle nought availeth, / The labor and the wounds are vain," Clough had written;

For while the tired waves, vainly breaking,
Seem here no painful inch to gain,
Far back, through creeks and inlets making,
Comes silent, flooding in, the main.

CHAPTER NINE

NO TINKLING BELLS

To be a good Nurse one must be a good woman, *or one is truly nothing but a tinkling bell.*

— Florence Nightingale

LORENCE NIGHTINGALE LIVED FOR MORE THAN FIFTY YEARS following her return from the nightmare of the Crimean War, but after Sidney Herbert's death she was an invalid. This woman who had worked so tirelessly for the health of others was now a slave to her own ailments. She was prone to fainting and weakness, and the sight of food turned her stomach. She was no longer strong enough to travel, go out to dinner, or even walk. When she moved from one home to another, she was carried in a chair borne with reverence by old soldiers, like an ancient queen – or a goddess.

She moved from the Burlington Hotel, with its sad memories, to an apartment in London, and later to a house owned by Sir Harry Verney. She lived alone, keeping her address secret. Sam Smith stood between her and the world, intercepting calls and letters. She avoided public appearances, and most visitors were turned away. Seeing Clarkey – or even the Queen of Holland – was "quite, quite, quite impossible," she said.

Bitter with loneliness and grief, she sank into self-pity. She complained that, instead of following her good example, other women remained useless and unfeeling. "Not one of my Crimean following learnt anything from me," she wrote to Clarkey. Women, she said, "scream at you for sympathy all day long, they are incapable of giving *any* in return." She set her own troubles above everyone else's, declaring that *she* was Sidney Herbert's "real widow" and Arthur Clough's "real widow" – never mind Elizabeth and Blanche. She said that she had developed "congestion of the spine, which could lead straight to paralysis."

If Florence was headed for paralysis, she was certainly taking the long way around. She had lost much of her power at the War Office, but the department still relied on her; she was the one who remembered everything, understood everything, knew where to find everything. She produced towers of paperwork on demand – notes, regulations, overviews, letters – all without pay. She wrote about medical equipment, shipboard diets, instructions for surgeons, treatments for yellow fever and cholera. She even came up with a cost-accounting system for the army's medical services.

In the spring of 1861, civil war had broken out in the United States, between the northern and southern states. The Secretary of War for the north had asked Florence for advice on organizing army hospitals and medical care. She had sprung into action, sending him cartons of information, and packing off similar material to volunteer organizations caring for the sick and wounded. (She would likely have helped the southern states too, but mail to the south was disrupted by the war, and she had no way to communicate with them.)

Later that year, after a clash between the northern states and a British ship, it looked as though Britain might enter the war. Since Canada still belonged to Britain, British troops were rushed to Canadian soil. The War Office asked Florence to examine the plans for feeding and clothing the soldiers, and keeping them healthy through the icy winter. She rewrote the plans in excruciating

Like the British, the Americans had not had female army nurses before the Civil War. Dorothea Dix was a stern, no-nonsense reformer who had spent years helping the poor, imprisoned, and mentally ill. A friend of the Liverpool reformer William Rathbone and a longtime admirer of Florence's work in the Crimea, Dix persuaded the north's War Department to let her set up an army nursing corps of women volunteers. Dragon Dix, as some of her nurses called her, demanded that her recruits be plain-looking and over thirty, and "sober, earnest, self-sacrificing and self-sustained; [able to] bear the presence of suffering and exercise entire self-control . . . calm, gentle, quiet, active, and steadfast in duty. . . ." They would wear plain brown or black, "with no bows, no curls, no jewelry, and no hoop skirts." Clearly a woman after Florence's own heart!

detail, considering everything from the speed of sleds over snow to the benefits of using buffalo robes in place of blankets. (As it turned out, Britain managed to stay out of the war.)

At the same time, she was keeping a sharp eye on the Nightingale Training School for Nurses. In 1859, she had remarked to Sidney Herbert that Sarah Wardroper – the matron (head nurse) of St. Thomas's Hospital, in London – was the only person she would trust to run a nursing school. In June 1860, supported by money from the Nightingale Fund, the school had opened its doors – on the premises of St. Thomas's, with Mrs. Wardroper as superintendent. She would run the school for twenty-seven years.

The probationers (students) signed up for a one-year course followed by three years of hospital practice. The course was based on the principles that Florence had stressed in her book *Notes on Nursing*. Sickrooms should be bright, clean, and airy. Water must be pure, and food must be wholesome. Nurses should be calm, discreet, and acutely sensitive to the moods and fears of their patients. There was no place for carelessness or uncleanliness, or meaningless chatter.

The probationers were carefully selected. Each would have her own room at St. Thomas's, not far from the apartment of the watchful Mrs. Wardroper. Living expenses would be paid by the Nightingale Fund, but Florence

PLAIN TALK AND COMMON SENSE

Notes on Nursing shows Florence's sharp tongue as well as her good sense:

Affectation, like whispering or walking on tip-toe, is peculiarly painful to the sick. An affectedly quiet voice, an affectedly sympathising voice, like an undertaker's at a funeral, sets all their nerves on edge. . . .

Do not meet or overtake a patient who is moving about in order to speak to him, or to give him any message or letter. You might just as well give him a box on the ear. I have seen a patient fall flat on the ground. . . . A patient in such a state is not going to the East Indies. If you would wait ten seconds, or walk ten yards further, any journey he could make would be over. . . .

Dusting in these days means nothing but flapping the dust from one part of a room on to another with doors and windows closed. What you do it for, I cannot think. The only way I know to *remove* dust . . . is to wipe everything with a damp cloth.

Sarah Wardroper had started nursing, with no training, when her husband died and she had to support her two children. (Her black mourning dress marks her as a widow.) She had become matron of St. Thomas's through hard work, determination, and high standards. Thanks to her, St. Thomas's had better nursing than any other hospital in London. According to Florence, Mrs. Wardroper's "whole heart and mind, her whole life and strength" were devoted to her work; it was no wonder the two women got along so well.

arranged to have books and flowers sent from Embley. The probationer's uniform consisted of a plain brown dress with a white cap and apron.

The students had to keep notebooks of their work, which could be inspected at any time. They also had to keep diaries. Florence reviewed the diaries once a month; after struggling to read some of them, she added spelling practice to the curriculum. As well as learning the hands-on skills of nursing, the probationers attended scientific lectures by doctors at the hospital, so that they would understand the diseases they were treating, and the cures they were helping to effect.

Day by day, there was more to learn. In 1864 a French microbiologist, Louis Pasteur, proved that infections did not "just happen," but were spread by tiny organisms in the air and elsewhere. The next year, Joseph Lister, a British surgeon, showed that if carbolic acid was put on wounds and dressings, and even sprayed around the operating room, fewer surgeries led to infection. Although some doctors still mocked the idea of germs – "Where are these little beasts?" hooted one professor – hospitals gradually adopted better hygiene, including rubber gloves, face masks, and sterilized instruments. As well, many hospitals were beginning to specialize in particular diseases – of the eyes, of the chest, of the skin. As specialists worked together and shared their discoveries, they quickly learned more about diagnosis and treatment.

Florence knew that any misbehavior by her nurses would discredit the school, and the whole idea of professional women nurses. Probationers were marked not only on their care of the sick (bandaging, bed-making, hygiene, medical notes, etc.) but on "Sobriety . . . Honesty . . . Truthfulness" and other virtues.

Not all the doctors at St. Thomas's were in favor of the nursing school. Some still felt that nurses were no more than housemaids, and needed no medical training. In *Notes on Nursing* Florence charged that "No *man*, not even a doctor, ever gives any other definition of what a nurse should be than this – 'devoted and obedient.' This definition would do just as well for a porter. It might even do for a horse."

But while she was often exasperated by men and their attitudes to women, she was not a strong supporter of the women's rights movement, which was

The probationers' dining room at St. Thomas's. Florence demanded a great deal from her students, but she also treated them to a life of comfort and dignity. The higher their own self-respect, the more easily they would win respect in the medical world. They were to be not just nurses but educators, passing on their high standards to the nurses around them.

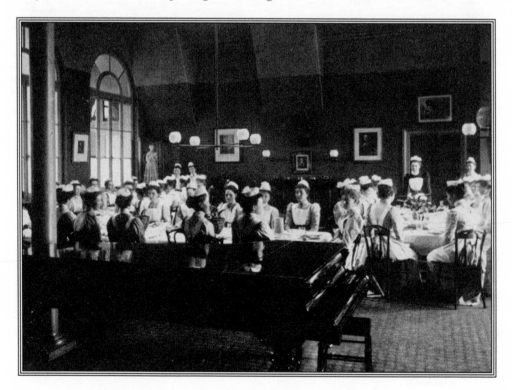

gaining strength at the time. Of course women should be able to vote – that was obvious – but the possibility was years away, and she saw more urgent issues to deal with. She was scornful of jargon "which urges women to do all that men do . . . merely because men do it," and equally scornful of that "which urges women to do nothing that men do, merely because they are women. . . ." Women, she declared, ought to do "the thing that is good whether it is suitable for a woman or not." Wasn't that what she had always done?

Thirteen probationers graduated from the first nursing class. They were registered as "certificated nurses," and began their hospital practice. Although the school would have some ups and downs, a new age of nursing had begun.

❧

Meanwhile, the British army remained very much on Florence's mind. Soldiers who were serving in India – which, like Canada, was still a British possession – died in appalling numbers. The main reason was poor sanitation. Badly placed latrines (toilets) and garbage dumps were polluting the air and water supply. Another reason was the blistering heat. Bacteria grew quickly in lukewarm food and water, and infections raced through the crowded, sweltering barracks.

Florence had been brooding for some time over the health of the army in India, and pressing for a Royal Commission on the subject. The commission had been authorized in 1859, and she had sent a questionnaire to every military base in India, asking about diet, clothing, climate, medical care, sanitation – everything she could think of. She had also written to every senior army and medical official, asking for facts and figures. The result was an entire roomful of documents, which she analyzed with the help of Dr. Sutherland and Dr. Farr, the statistician.

The official report on the health of the troops in India, published in 1863, was over two thousand pages long. It was crammed with details, most of them supplied by Florence, and included a section of twenty-three pages written by Florence herself, and illustrated (at Florence's expense) by Hilary Bonham

Carter. It was very impressive – but only members of Parliament were allowed to have it. For everyone else the government prepared a shorter version, leaving out the embarrassing bits. This time the cover-up didn't work. Florence published the section she had written, including Hilary's pictures, and – as usual – sent it to the Queen and anyone else who might read it.

The result was another scandal. British soldiers were living in disgusting quarters, drinking filthy water, consoling themselves with gambling and drunkenness. Military hospitals stank from garbage and pollution, and the beds were so loaded with blood-sucking insects that patients could hardly sleep. But the problem wasn't limited to the troops. There were more than 200

Hilary Bonham Carter's view of British soldiers in India, smoking and gambling and living an unhealthy life. Her vivid sketches helped Florence gain popular support for sanitary reform in India.

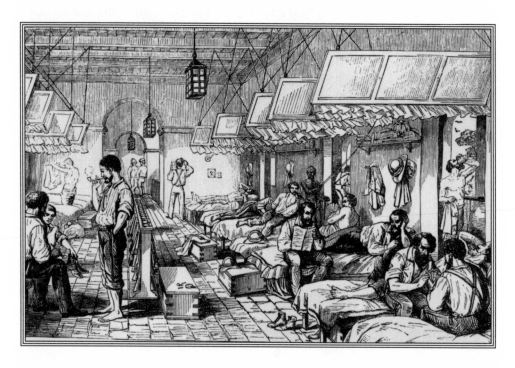

million people in India, and most of them had miserable living conditions. The only way to keep the soldiers well was to improve the health of the local population. Undaunted by the challenge, Florence drew up a plan for a public health service for the entire country.

Sir John Lawrence, who had just been named viceroy (Queen's representative) of India, came to visit Florence. He was a strong-willed man of deep religious convictions. He had served in India for almost thirty years, and spoke several local languages. He agreed with her proposals, and when he got back to India he did his best to set reforms in motion. A stream of letters connected India's viceregal palace to the modest bedroom in north London.

Clearly the people of India must have clean water and proper sewage systems, and decent hospitals and medical care. But they couldn't be healthy without food, so Florence looked into improving the farming system as well. She worked out better ways to irrigate the dry soil. She pressed her views on the bureaucrats who ran the Indian administration from the safety and comfort of England. She wrote pamphlets, academic papers, and newspaper articles. She even wrote an educational booklet for the elders of Indian villages, which was translated into Bengali, Gujarati, and other Indian languages. Benjamin Jowett christened her "Governess of the Governor of India." No, replied Florence, just "Maid of all (Dirty) Work."

Like Sidney Herbert, Lawrence and his successors never accomplished nearly as much as they hoped to. India is a vast country; the religious and political situation was extremely complicated; the cost of the reforms would have been staggering. Florence's great plans were not fulfilled, but at least the work was begun. Thirty years after that first meeting with Lawrence, she would still be pushing for better conditions in India.

❧

She was dealing with a hundred other concerns as well. She was still sorting out problems at the Army Medical School. As the army improved its barracks and hospitals, she reviewed the building plans and noted every mistake. She even demanded windows in the army stables so the horses could see out. (But there *were* some windows, high up, teased Dr. Sutherland; the horses had only to stand on their hind legs to enjoy the view.)

Florence was also concerned about the dangers of childbirth. Earlier generations of mothers had given birth in their homes, helped by midwives who had learned their skills by apprenticing. By the 1850s, many babies were being born in hospitals, where doctors could offer painkillers, anesthetics, and other new inventions. There was just one problem: mothers and infants often caught fatal diseases in these hospitals.

Florence used some money from the Nightingale Fund to open a school for village midwives. The women were given six months' training in how to deliver babies in the safety of the family home. The school operated for six years, but then it closed, partly because of an outbreak of childbed (puerperal) fever.

Florence then turned her attention to childbirth in hospitals. She and Dr. Sutherland collected statistics from doctors, hospitals, and health authorities, and proved that a woman who had a baby in an institution was far more likely to die than one who gave birth in her own home, however humble it might be. The bigger the hospital, the higher the death rate. No woman having a baby, she declared, "should ever pass the doors of a general hospital."

In 1861, William Rathbone – a wealthy shipowner from Liverpool who was dedicated to charitable projects and social reform – asked Florence where he could find visiting nurses to help poor, sick people in their own homes. She advised him to start a nursing school. He did so, at his own expense, and soon Liverpool was graduating classfuls of nurses taught according to Nightingale principles.

But that was only the beginning. Many homeless, penniless people lived in "workhouse" institutions, where they received the bare necessities of life and did whatever jobs could be found for them. Often, though, they were

Agnes Jones was thirty-two when she was chosen to be matron of the nurses at the Liverpool workhouse infirmary. Despite the horrors she found there, she wrote to Florence that "I am happier than I have ever been in one of the happiest lives, I suppose, anyone was ever allowed to live." A happy life, perhaps, but a short one; four years later she caught typhus and died.

penniless because they *couldn't* work – because they were very young or very old, or physically or mentally ill. In that case they often ended up in the workhouse infirmary (hospital). Rathbone had found that more than a thousand people were living in the infirmary of Liverpool's workhouse, with no medical care and almost no sanitation. He wanted to hire Nightingale nurses to help them.

Florence dispatched a dozen nurses to Liverpool, under the command of Sir John Lawrence's niece, an experienced nurse named Agnes Jones. The conditions they found there were appalling. The wards were filthy. There was almost no food, but plenty of liquor, so drunkenness and vile behavior prevailed. Before long, though, the Nightingale nurses had the infirmary operating to decent standards. The grateful Rathbone sent Florence a flower-stand, and kept it stocked with plants for the rest of his life.

Florence resolved to improve workhouse infirmaries across the country. She wanted changes in the way they were organized and financed, and she wanted children, sick people, incurable people, and the mentally ill housed separately, according to their needs. But this would require new laws. Using her influence on Lord Palmerston, she almost got what she wanted – but then Palmerston died, the bill was delayed, and the government was defeated. The Metropolitan Poor Act was finally passed in 1867. It was much less than she wanted, but it was a start, and more would come. In the meantime she campaigned for emigration, to move poor people from Britain's foul, crowded slums to the spacious lands of North America.

Through all of this, her own losses continued. In December 1861, just six months after Sidney Herbert died, death claimed another of her most valuable supporters. Prince Albert succumbed to typhoid fever at the age of forty-two. Devastated by grief, Queen Victoria retreated into deep mourning for the rest of her life. "The Widow of Windsor" became almost as much a recluse as Florence.

In 1865, Hilary Bonham Carter died of cancer. After Florence had sent her cousin off to work on her art, other relatives had nibbled away at Hilary's time – "like Fleas," said Clarkey. Unlike Florence, the talented artist had never managed to escape the demands of her home and family.

In the fall of 1865, Florence moved into a small London house of her own, bought for her (rather grudgingly) by her father. She was forty-five years old. She was still suffering heart problems, and now she had dreadful back pains as well. Injections of morphia (opium), an addictive drug that was dangerously overused in Victorian times, relieved the pain but sometimes made her too groggy to concentrate. She hoped that in her new home, with a house full of cats and a garden full of birds, she would find some comfort for her misery.

FULL CIRCLE

The way to live with God is to live with Ideals, not merely to think about ideals, but to do and suffer for them.

– Florence Nightingale

T IS A MYSTERY HOW FLORENCE NIGHTINGALE MANAGED to impose her will in so many areas. She was born into an age that wanted her to be submissive and retiring, into a class that wanted her to be decorative and amusing. She had no wealth of her own, no title, no university degrees, and – except for her two years in the Crimea – no government authority. She was mild-mannered, physically slight, frequently ill. Yet, like the steam driving a steam engine, her relentless determination powered new achievements in one direction after another.

And here's another mystery: what exactly was wrong with her health? Why was she always complaining of weakness, dizziness, nausea, a pounding heart? Did she have a physical disorder, or was all this from mental stress? Was she unconsciously slipping into the Victorian role of a "delicate lady" overwhelmed by emotion? Or was poor health just one more tool she could use to get her own way?

It's been suggested that she had brucellosis, an infection caught from farm animals. Or post-traumatic stress disorder (a disturbed mental condition), set off by her horrifying experiences in the Crimean War. Or a rare heart condition, or various other ailments. But it seems more likely that her desperate frustration – at her family, at social conventions, at bureaucratic stupidity – caused her breathlessness and racing heart, which in turn caused weakness and nausea. We know now that a fast heartbeat is often caused by anxiety or stress; usually it has nothing to do with heart disease. But in those days doctors thought a fast heartbeat was a sign of a dangerous ailment, so they ordered Florence to stay in bed – which only made things worse. Unable to "blow off steam" physically, she converted her fury into paperwork. In her lifetime she wrote about thirteen thousand letters, and published some two hundred books, pamphlets, and papers.

By the time she was in her late forties, though, she was slowing down. Perhaps she was too tired to keep going. Perhaps, as she aged, she accepted the fact that there were limits to what she could do. Or perhaps the drugs that relieved her pain also damped the fire that had burned so fiercely. Whatever the reason, by the middle of her life she had completed most of her work, and was beginning a slow progress into old age.

In 1866 she spent some time with her mother, at Embley. Her father had business at Lea Hurst, and Fanny, who was almost eighty and going blind, was not well enough to go with him. As for Parthe – Lady Verney – she was now a society hostess, and she painted and wrote stories and essays as well. She was much too busy to go.

It was Florence's first stay at Embley in many years, and she found her mother a great deal easier to deal with – "so much gentler, calmer, more thoughtful," she told Clarkey. Unfortunately, no one could say the same of Florence. She was disapproving and critical, and nobody dared argue with her because of her famous "heart condition."

After she returned to London, she continued working but retreated to Malvern from time to time, to rest and recover her strength. In 1868 she stayed with her parents for three months, at Lea Hurst. She and Fanny got along better during this visit, and Florence found time to read Shakepeare's plays and Jane Austen's novels. She began spending a few months every year at either Embley or Lea Hurst.

⊰⊱

In 1870, Europe was once again caught up in fighting, in the Franco-Prussian War. The enemies were France, on one side, and Prussia and other German states, on the other. Britain was not involved.

Hospitals improved dramatically during Florence's lifetime. Note the open windows, fresh flowers, and spotless bedding in this roomy children's ward in Guy's Hospital, London, and the carefully pleated napkin tucked into the handle of the washing jug.

By this time, there was a new international agreement to aid sick and wounded troops. In 1862, a Swiss businessman named Henri Dunant had written a book about the dreadful sufferings of wounded soldiers. He had called for volunteers from all countries to help them. He had urged that people doing this lifesaving work be treated not as enemies, but as "neutrals" who must not be attacked by either side.

Dunant's appeal had far-reaching effects. Soon a dozen nations had signed the Geneva Convention, promising (among other things) to respect the safety of one another's medical workers. People helping the wounded would be identified by a red cross on a white background – the flag of Switzerland, with the colors reversed.

National groups were set up to arrange hospitals, medical workers, and materials, and to collect money for all this. Although Florence refused an executive role in the British group – she was too busy working on sanitary reform for India – Sir Harry Verney and Dr. Sutherland were both involved and, as usual, everyone turned to Florence as the expert. She was consulted on practical matters of all kinds, and she helped to select volunteers, raise funds, and organize supplies. Strangers sent her money to help the wounded, knowing that she would put it to good use. "Every man and woman in the world," she griped to Clarkey, "seems to have come into it with the express purpose of writing to me." The French and the Prussians both asked for her advice on hospitals and procedures, and she sent Nightingale nurses to help the wounded in both armies. After the war, she received medals from both sides.

These national groups eventually grew into today's Red Cross and Red Crescent societies, which help people stricken by war and other disasters. When Dunant was praised for his role in this tremendous humanitarian project, he said modestly that he had been inspired by Florence's work in Scutari; "all the honour of [the Geneva] Convention" was hers.

At home, medicine itself was a battlefield, as women fought for the right to be physicians. First they had to win admittance to medical schools; then they needed legal recognition. In the United States, Elizabeth Blackwell managed to get into medical school; she graduated in 1849 and opened a New York women's hospital in 1857. Two years later she became the first female doctor registered in Britain. Blackwell, who knew Florence and agreed with her ideas about hygiene, started the first American nursing school in 1861, and trained members of Dorothea Dix's Army Nursing Corps during the Civil War. In 1874 a women's medical college opened in London, with Dr. Blackwell as a professor. A lot of medical schools continued to refuse women, but at least the women now had some route into the profession.

⁂

By 1872, Florence had to accept the fact that she had lost her influence in matters concerning India and the army. A new government, with different priorities, had been in power for several years. Many of the officials who respected her knowledge had retired or died, and their replacements saw no need to discuss business with a middle-aged invalid lady, however famous. For years she had worked frantically, convinced that death would snatch her away before she could finish. Now here she was, very much alive, and what was left for her to do?

For a while she talked of retiring to a bed in a public ward at St. Thomas's, among the poor patients. Since she was no longer doing anything useful, she said, she had no right to cost her father so much money. Jowett managed to talk her out of this melodramatic notion, and her next plan was to move nearer to St. Thomas's and reorganize the nursing school. But she ended up living with her parents instead. They were no longer able to manage their own affairs, and someone had to take charge. Florence was once again mired in the household trivia she had escaped so long before, and it was just as infuriating and time-wasting as ever. "Oh to be turned back to this petty stagnant stifling life at Embley," she wrote.

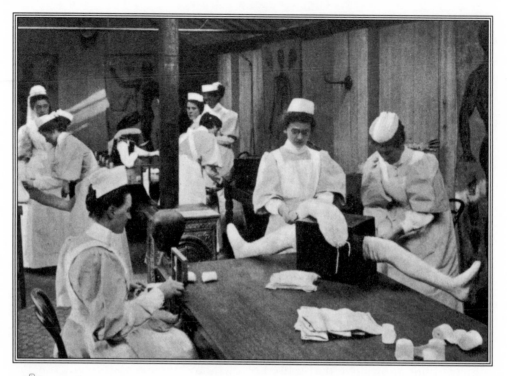

Student nurses practice bandaging techniques in 1906. By this time there were nursing schools based on Florence's system in twenty countries around the world. Looking at these diligent professionals, it's hard to believe that, just fifty years earlier, most nurses had been despised as immoral drunkards.

She found her mind turning more and more to religion and philosophy, to the question of what life was all about. Encouraged by Benjamin Jowett, she had been reading theological books, and had published several essays of religious philosophy. She had helped Jowett with a children's edition of the Bible, and with translating Plato from classical Greek. She began working on a book of religious mysticism, translating passages from authors of the Middle Ages. At times, her meditations led her back to the feelings of guilt and worthlessness that had tormented her long ago.

In early 1874, Florence's father died. He had inherited his wealth from an uncle, and under the terms of his uncle's will, because William Nightingale had no male heirs, Embley Park now passed to his nephew – Mai Smith's son, Shore. By this time Fanny was totally blind, and her mind had retreated to earlier, happier days. It was impossible for her to remain at Embley after the Smith family took over the house; Aunt Mai was old and crippled, and Uncle Sam was an invalid. Florence had to remove her poor mother to Lea Hurst, and live there with her. She had to organize the move, and hire new servants, and get the household up and running. She who had managed a thousand patients, and more, now spent her days caring for one frail, befuddled, helpless old woman.

In 1879, Florence wrote Clarkey that the five years since her father's death had been the hardest of her life. She was monitoring her nursing school as closely as she could. She wrote pamphlets about nursing care for the poor, and advised William Rathbone on setting up a city nursing association. She was still investigating the problems in India, devising solutions through irrigation, land reform, and education. But she had to do everything through letters, which was maddeningly slow and inefficient. Yet however trapped and miserable she felt, she couldn't bring herself to abandon her mother.

But the next year Fanny died, and Florence was released from her domestic duties. Queen Victoria – now Empress of India – wrote her a letter of sympathy. Florence sent the Queen a lecture on the miseries of the Indian people.

❧

Back in London, Florence began to find peace and even serenity. Like the finest of hospital wards, her house was spotlessly clean and airy, and bright with flowers. Shore Smith was paying her a very generous allowance. She had half a dozen maids caring for her, and a retired soldier ran her errands. She treated herself to small but exquisite meals, specifying every detail of the preparations. She entertained the children of her friends and relatives, and enjoyed sending them little treats and surprises. When she wasn't working,

🐝 *As she grew older, Florence spent her days on a couch or a bed, reading and writing, dressed in black silk with a shawl draped over her feet, and a white scarf of net or lace covering her hair.*

she fed the birds on her balcony, and played with her family of Persian cats.

Her house was near the Verneys' London home, and she saw her sister and brother-in-law often. She also went to stay at Claydon House, their beautiful country mansion. Parthe had become badly crippled by arthritis, so Florence helped run the house, and planned improvements in the sanitation of nearby villages. The two sisters were getting along well now, and Florence treasured Harry Verney's company; they spent hours in thoughtful discussion. After Sam Smith died, she finally made up with her long-suffering Aunt Mai.

She was no longer tormented, no longer longing for death. "I crave for it less," she wrote to Clarkey. "I want to do a little work, a little better, before I die." As it happened, more work was soon coming her way. There had been another change of government, and Florence was again consulted regularly – about hospitals, about the army, about public health, about India.

She found enormous satisfaction in her Nightingale nurses. She interviewed every probationer, not only assessing the behavior and character of each student, but also listening seriously to any suggestions about the school. She laid out a course of general reading for the women, and made sure they were encouraged to enjoy poetry and music, and to attend church. Her school, she wrote, must be "a place of training of character, habits and intelligence, as well as of acquiring knowledge."

She stayed in touch with many of the nurses long after they graduated and took up posts in Britain and abroad. She sent them flowers, money, and other comforts. When they were sick she arranged seaside holidays, or invited them to visit. They were the children she had never had; they were her pets, her immortality, her gift to future generations. Her letters to them were often affectionate, even maternal. At the same time, she was always careful, as one biographer noted, "to hold up before her nurses' eyes the spiritual nature of their vocation, to instill into them not only the high standard of efficiency on which she was adamant but a sense of the presence of God."

Florence had done less than she wanted for the army, less than she wanted for Britain's poor, less than she wanted for the people of India – but her nurses? There they were, by the hundreds: resolute and professional, renowned for their skills and virtues. With their help, nursing schools had been founded in North America, Australia, and Scandinavia, and Nightingale power was working its magic in hospitals around the world.

In the 1880s, British troops were fighting in Egypt and the Sudan, in North Africa. (One of the issues was control of the valuable Suez Canal, Britain's shortcut to India.) Florence helped choose the party of nurses, led by a

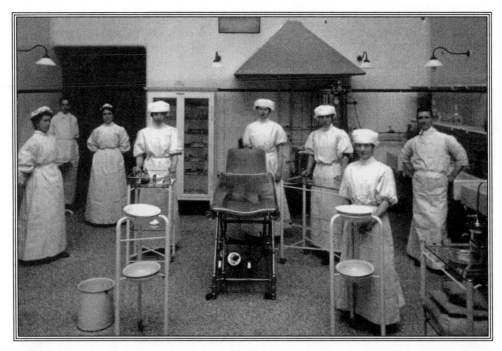

Surgical nurses in St. Thomas's operating room. Gone were the blood-crusted coats and filthy instruments. With decent hygiene, anesthetics, and antiseptics, and the development of better surgical tools, surgery was becoming a reasonable form of treatment, instead of a desperate last resort.

Nightingale matron, that would sail for Egypt. When it turned out that the army hospitals had problems of organization and supply – "It is the Crimea all over again," said Florence – she assisted in an official inquiry. When a regiment of soldiers arrived home from Egypt in 1882, she even ventured out to a few public events in their honor. The next year, Queen Victoria presented her with a new award – the Royal Red Cross Medal – for her achievements in military nursing. Florence thanked the Queen with a lengthy letter about the army medical services – and another letter about reform in India.

In 1887 a great jubilee celebrated the first fifty years of Queen Victoria's reign. In a curious replaying of history, the people of the British Empire donated money to honor the Queen, and – like Florence – the Queen used the funds to start a nursing institute: the Queen Victoria Jubilee Institute for Nurses. Like Florence, the Queen designed a uniform for her nurses, and took great interest in their progress. These women would be visiting nurses, going into poor people's homes to care for them. Florence didn't entirely approve of the new nurses – the selection and training were not as strict as she would have liked – but the Jubilee Institute was another important development in nursing.

By now, most of her old friends and relatives had died. Gone were Clarkey, the Bracebridges, Richard Monckton Milnes, Aunt Mai, and Dr. Farr. In 1890, Parthe died, and the next year Florence lost her most devoted workmate, Dr. Sutherland. In 1893, Benjamin Jowett – source of so much strength and comfort – was taken from her, and a few months later she lost Harry Verney, and then her dear cousin Shore Smith. And still Florence lived on, slower and more weary now, but with a peace of mind she had never known before.

Finally, finally, the Indian reforms were coming to pass. Projects of irrigation and sanitation were under way. Education was improving, and village leaders had been given more power to protect the rights of their communities. Florence watched every step of the proceedings, reviewing government papers, conferring with Indian visitors, and pressing for more and more progress.

The nineteenth century was drawing to a close, and the leisurely, traditional life that Florence had been born into had almost disappeared. As the years went by, changes and inventions had come faster and faster. Telephones were ringing in some homes now, and electric lightbulbs were glowing, and recorded music played on the phonograph. Inventors were tinkering with a host of appliances that would soon replace servants. Automobiles were starting to chug down the roads and laneways. Two American brothers, the bicycle mechanics Wilbur and Orville Wright, were refining their plans for a flying machine. Two French brothers named Lumière were turning still pictures into silent movies.

A physicist named Marconi was experimenting with radio waves. A scientist couple, Marie and Pierre Curie, had discovered a radioactive element called radium. A scientist named Mach was working on a theory of supersonic speed. An inventor named Hollerith had built an early calculator that read holes punched in cards, and had started a company that would grow into IBM. Around the world, researchers were exploring dazzling new prospects. They could hardly imagine the world that would grow out of their discoveries, within the space of a few generations.

In 1901 the Victorian era came to an end, when the aged queen finally went to join her beloved, long-lost Albert. In that same year, Florence – who had achieved so much through her reading and writing – became blind. She hired a companion to read to her, but not for long. By 1907, when King Edward VII sent her the Order of Merit – a medal that had never before been granted to a woman – her mind was no longer capable of understanding the honor. She spent a few more years wandering, lost in her own mind, and died peacefully on August 13, 1910.

Florence Nightingale. For many people the name still conjures up the image that was so popular a hundred and fifty years ago: the sweet, patient angel of mercy. The real Florence was a difficult, demanding woman. She was driven by frustration, by resentment – most of all, perhaps, by outrage at the wrongness she saw around her: the stupendous gulf between the way life ought to be, and the way life was.

She could have thrown up her hands in helplessness. She could have tsk-tsked at the army, tut-tutted at the government, brushed the cake crumbs off her skirt, and rung for another pot of tea. After all, she was a Victorian lady. It wasn't her job to fix the world.

Instead, she turned the force of her feelings into energy, and set out to correct *everything*. She accepted no excuses, allowed no compromises. As Mrs. Gaskell had once said, Florence's heart and soul were absorbed by her work. If she didn't always succeed, at least she always tried.

Benjamin Jowett had reminded Florence, thirty years before she died, that "nobody knows how many lives are saved by your nurses in hospitals (you have introduced a new era in nursing): how many thousand soldiers who would have fallen victim to bad air, bad drainage and ventilation, are now alive owing to your forethought and diligence; how many natives of India . . . have been preserved from famine, oppression and the load of debt. . . ." By acting, by teaching, by writing and persuading and arguing, she had made an astonishing contribution.

What angel could have done more?

✺ *(Next page) Florence Nightingale had wanted her body donated for medical research. The government offered her family a grand ceremony and burial at Westminster Abbey, alongside kings and queens. The compromise was a quiet country funeral. In London, dignitaries attended a memorial service at St. Paul's Cathedral, and thousands of nurses and ex-soldiers flocked to honor her.* Bottom left: *This old soldier showed up in his uniform from the Crimea.* Bottom center: *One of her Crimean patients stands by her grave, near Embley Park. The monument bears inscriptions she wrote for her parents and for Parthe; for herself there are only her initials and the dates of her birth and death.*

SOURCE NOTES

Publisher and date are given where a book is first referred to, unless the book is a classic or is included in the Selected Bibliography. All quotes from Florence Nightingale and her family are drawn directly from their papers, or are cited in Cecil Woodham-Smith, *Florence Nightingale: 1820–1910*, or Barbara Montgomery Dossey, *Florence Nightingale: Mystic, Visionary, Healer*.

CHAPTER 1

The epigraph is from Isaac Watts, *Divine and Moral Songs for Children* (R.T.S., n.d.), cited in Nigel Temple, *Seen and Not Heard: A Garland of Fancies for Victorian Children* (New York: Dial, 1970). The Charles Dickens quote is from *Hard Times*. The comment on the dangers of stage coaches was made by Pitt Lennox, and is cited in J.B. Priestley, *The Prince of Pleasure and His Regency 1811–1820*.

CHAPTER 2

The epigraph is from the Rev. David Blair, *The Mother's Question Book, Containing Things Necessary to be Known at an Early Age* (Darton: n.d.), cited in Nigel Temple, *Seen and Not Heard*. The Jane Austen quotes "All young ladies" and "all the Metals" are from *Pride and Prejudice* and *Mansfield Park*, respectively. *The Mysteries of Udolpho* was written by Ann Radcliffe, and first published in 1794.

CHAPTER 3

The epigraph is from Lytton Strachey, *Eminent Victorians*, as is the description of a nurse as "a coarse old woman." The Mary Clarke quotes "Why don't they talk" and "faddling twaddling," are cited in Cecil Woodham-Smith, *Florence Nightingale*, as are the Thackeray and Carlyle quotes, and the quote from the "famous American social reformer" (Dr. Ward Howe).

CHAPTER 4

The lines by Alfred, Lord Tennyson are from *The Princess*. The story of the Vienna doctor (Ignaz Semmelweis) tracking childbed fever is drawn from Roy Porter, *The Greatest Benefit to Mankind*.

CHAPTER 5

The epigraph is from Lytton Strachey, *Eminent Victorians*. The Gaskell quote is cited in Elizabeth Haldane, *Mrs. Gaskell and Her Friends* (Freeport, NY: Books for Libraries, 1970). The *Times* article was by William Russell and is cited in Cecil Woodham-Smith, *Florence Nightingale*, as are the letters from Herbert and Monckton Milnes, and the nurse's complaint about the cap. The Fenton quote is from Roger Fenton, *Roger Fenton: Photographer of the Crimean War* (London: Secker & Warburg, 1954).

CHAPTER 6

The epigraph is cited in Cecil Woodham-Smith, *Florence Nightingale*. Russell's description of the Charge of the Light Brigade is from William Russell, *Russell's Despatches from the Crimea*; the description of Constantinople is also his, from the same source. The lines by Alfred, Lord Tennyson are from "The Charge of the Light Brigade." The sergeant's quote is from T. Gowing, *A Voice from the Ranks: A Personal Narrative of the Crimean Campaign*, ed. K. Fenwick, 1954, cited in J.B. Priestley, *Victoria's Heyday*. The Victorian biographer is Lytton Strachey, writing in *Eminent Victorians*; this is also the source of the quotation beginning "by strict method." The remarks "Nightingale power," "If she were at our head," and "But it must be done" are cited in Cecil Woodham-Smith, *Florence Nightingale*, as are the quotes from Charles Bracebridge and Queen Victoria. The quote from the steamer commander is cited in Lawrence James, *Crimea, 1854–56: The War with Russia from Contemporary Photographs* (New York: Van Nostrand Reinhold, 1981).

CHAPTER 7

The epigraph is cited in J.B. Priestley, *Victoria's Heyday*. "You are spoiling the brutes" and "dishonest, extravagant" are cited in Cecil Woodham-Smith, *Florence Nightingale*, as are the lyrics "May God give her strength," the statement from the War Department, and the quotes from Soyer and Queen Victoria. The anagram is cited in Barbara Montgomery Dossey, *Florence Nightingale*. The Gaskell quote is from Elizabeth Haldane, *Mrs. Gaskell and Her Friends*.

CHAPTER 8

The Palmerston and Sutherland quotes are cited in Cecil Woodham-Smith, *Florence Nightingale*. The lines by Arthur Clough are from "Say Not the Struggle Nought Availeth." The quote about crinolines is from Daniel Pool, *What Jane Austen Ate and Charles Dickens Knew*. The story of the Malvern doctor is drawn from Sir George White Pickering, *Creative Malady: Illness in the Lives and Minds of Charles Darwin, Florence Nightingale, Mary Baker Eddy, Sigmund Freud, Marcel Proust, Elizabeth Barrett Browning* (London: Allen & Unwin, 1974). The story of Mary, Lady Verney is drawn from Antonia Fraser, *The Weaker Vessel* (New York: Knopf, 1984).

CHAPTER 9

The Dorothea Dix quotes are cited in Dorothy Clarke Wilson, *Stranger and Traveler*. The quote "Where are the little beasts?" is from John Hughes Bennett, and is cited in Roy Porter, *The Greatest Benefit to Mankind*. The quotes from Jowett and Clarke are cited in Cecil Woodham-Smith, *Florence Nightingale*, and that from Jones is cited in Elspeth Huxley, *Florence Nightingale*.

CHAPTER 10

Many of the comments on Florence Nightingale's health are based on Sir George White Pickering, *Creative Malady*. The Dunant quote is cited in Dorothy Clarke Wilson, *Stranger and Traveler*. The quote "to hold up . . ." is from biographer Cecil Woodham-Smith, and appears in Cecil Woodham-Smith, *Florence Nightingale*, as does the Jowett quote.

SELECTED BIBLIOGRAPHY

Dossey, Barbara Montgomery. *Florence Nightingale: Mystic, Visionary, Healer.* Springhouse, PA: Springhouse, 1999.

Huxley, Elspeth. *Florence Nightingale.* London: Weidenfeld & Nicolson, 1975.

Nightingale, Florence. *Notes on Hospitals.* London: Longman, Green, Longman, Roberts, and Green, 1863.

———. *Notes on Nursing for the Labouring Classes.* London: Harrison, 1868.

Pool, Daniel. *What Jane Austen Ate and Charles Dickens Knew: From Fox-Hunting to Whist – the Facts of Daily Life in 19th-Century England.* New York: Simon & Schuster, 1993.

Porter, Roy. *The Greatest Benefit to Mankind: A Medical History of Humanity from Antiquity to the Present.* London: Fontana, 1999.

Priestley, J.B. *The Prince of Pleasure and His Regency 1811–1820.* London: Sphere, 1971.

———. *Victoria's Heyday.* Harmondsworth: Penguin, 1972.

Russell, William Howard. *Russell's Despatches from the Crimea.* Ed. by Nicolas Bentley. London: Panther, 1970.

Strachey, Lytton. *Eminent Victorians: The Illustrated Edition.* London: Bloomsbury, 1988.

Wilson, Dorothy Clarke. *Stranger and Traveler: The Story of Dorothea Dix, American Reformer.* Boston: Little, Brown, 1975.

Woodham-Smith, Cecil. *Florence Nightingale: 1820–1910.* New York: Atheneum, 1983.

PICTURE SOURCES

Every reasonable effort has been made to trace the ownership of copyright materials. Any information allowing the publisher to correct a reference or credit in future will be welcomed. Pictures not attributed are from the author's collection.

For space reasons the following abbreviations have been used:

FNM   The Florence Nightingale Museum Trust, London, U.K.
LMA   London Metropolitan Archives, London, U.K.
LOC   Library of Congress, Washington D.C., U.S.A.
TRL   Toronto Reference Library, Toronto, Canada
WIL   Wellcome Institute Library, London, U.K.

Page 5: reproduced by permission of Sir Ralph Verney, photograph from Photographic Survey, Courtauld Institute of Art (neg. L96/23[27]); 6: courtesy of FNM (0001); 8: *The North Country Mails at the Peacock, Islington,* by James Pollard, Yale Center for British Art, Paul Mellon Collection (B1981.25.506); 9: *Rolling Mills at Merthyr Tydfil,* by T. Horner, courtesy of The National Museum of Wales (NMWA 3353); 14, 16, 18: TRL; 20: Royal Institute of British Architects Library, Early Imprints Collection; 22, 26, 28: TRL; 31: *Richard Monckton Milnes, 1st Baron Houghton,* by George Richmond, by courtesy of the National Portrait Gallery, London, U.K. (3824); 33: *An apothecary, John Simmonds, and his boy apprentice . . . ,* J.G. Murray, after W. Hunt, courtesy of WIL (V0010844B00); 39: *Monster Soup, commonly called Thames Water,* by William Heath, courtesy of WIL (L0006579B00); 41: from *Illustrated Times,* courtesy of WIL (L0001380B00); 44: courtesy of FNM (0009); 55: TRL; 58-59: VISU*TronX*; 61: courtesy of FNM; 62: courtesy of the Director, National Army Museum, London, U.K. (23526); 63:

TRL; 67: courtesy of FNM (0010); 69: TRL; 70: courtesy of FNM (0128.1); 73: by Robert Hooke, courtesy of WIL (M0016995B00); 75: TRL; 76: LOC (LC-USZ62-16452); 78, 82: TRL; 84: courtesy of FNM (0382.6); 86: courtesy of WIL (L0000029B00); 89, 93: LOC (LC-USZ62-75815, LC-USZ62-5877); 97: courtesy of WIL (V0047626B00); 99: courtesy of FNM (0821.1); 103: TRL; 106, 114: courtesy of FNM (0189, 0486); 115: courtesy of FNM, photograph courtesy of LMA (H1/ST/NCph/DI/6/3b[i]); 116: courtesy of FNM, photograph courtesy of LMA (H1/ST/NCph/CIV/e/15[iii]); 118, 121: courtesy of FNM (0934.1, 0495); 125: courtesy of King's College, London, photograph courtesy of LMA (H9/GYph/2/21/1); 128, 130: courtesy of WIL (L0001004B00, M0009131B00); 132: courtesy of FNM, photograph courtesy of LMA (H1/ST/NCph/CIV/b/77[iii]); 136: courtesy of FNM (0892).

ACKNOWLEDGMENTS

My thanks to Kathy Lowinger, publisher of Tundra Books, for suggesting that I write about Florence Nightingale. I imagined that the Lady with the Lamp would give me a change of pace after my books about firefighters and escaping slaves. I know now that this Victorian heroine would have made short work of a blazing building or a pack of slave-hunting dogs.

I am grateful to the many curators and archivists who helped me with facts and illustrations. In particular, London's Wellcome Trust is a researcher's dream, phenomenally well organized and accessible; thank you, Michele Minto.

Anyone who wants to feel close to the founder of modern nursing should try to get to London, where the Florence Nightingale Museum – by St. Thomas's Hospital, just across the river from Big Ben – weaves articles of her work and life into the memorial she deserves. The knowledge and patience of Alex Attewell, the curator, were invaluable to me. For more on the museum, see www.florence-nightingale.co.uk.

Special thanks, as ever, to my editor, Beverley Beetham Endersby.

INDEX